Healing Your Soul: Don't Let Your Past Hurts Destroy Your Future is a profound and transformative guide authored by Patti Hathaway and Keren Anderson. This book is a beacon of hope for those who have experienced deep wounds and traumas, offering a path to healing and liberation through the power of Christ.

In a world where the scars of pornography, satanic ritual abuse, narcissism, and spiritual oppression run deep, Hathaway and Anderson provide a roadmap to redemption. Their insights are both practical and deeply spiritual, guiding readers through the process of inner healing and freedom.

What sets this book apart is its unflinching exploration of complex issues such as the religious spirit, Jezebel, and Leviathan. The authors dismantle these spiritual strongholds with compassion and wisdom, empowering readers to reclaim their true identity in Christ. *Healing Your Soul* is not just a book—it's a journey of self-discovery and spiritual victory.

Through heartfelt storytelling, biblical teachings, and practical exercises, Hathaway and Anderson lead readers toward a deeper understanding of their soul and spirit. I wholeheartedly endorse *Healing Your Soul* to anyone seeking healing and freedom from the wounds of the past. May this book be a source of comfort, guidance, and empowerment on your journey toward wholeness in Christ.

Dr. Brian Simmons
Passion & Fire Ministries

Healing
Your Soul

Don't Let Your Past Hurts
Destroy Your Future

by Patti Hathaway, M.Ed.
Keren Anderson

www.SoulHealingCourses.com

Name_____

Healing Your Soul: Don't Let Your Past Hurts Destroy Your Future

By Patti Hathaway, M.Ed.
Keren Anderson

Published By:
www.SoulHealingCourses.com
Columbus, Ohio
USA

ISBN: 978-0-9904763-4-4

Library of Congress Cataloguing-in-Publication Data
Hathaway, Patti

Healing Your Soul: Don't Let Your Past Hurts Destroy Your Future

Healing Your Soul

Lessons

Overview

This book was originally co-authored with Dr. Sandy Burkett and published in 2010 as *Breakthrough Living: Healing Your Wounds That Hold You Back*. With 14 years of experience using this content, I expanded it to include two additional lessons on Soul Ties and In Utero Trauma that I found important to include for people impacted by past hurts of all sorts. In the end, I added about 100 pages of new content and testimonies. The result was *Healing Your Soul: Don't Let Your Past Hurts Destroy Your Future* which was published in 2021.

In 2024, I worked with my soul healing colleague Keren Anderson to completely re-write two lessons and add a lot of her Holy Spirit designed tools in the other lessons. She wrote the final *Walking in Victory* lesson 9. Our specific purpose is to use this book to create an eLearning course so that people can attend our course and do soul healing in the eLearning. Both of us are now running humanitarian foundations so we have very limited availability to minister to individual clients.

We are both involved in training and certifying Soul Healing Discipler Coaches who will be available to walk alongside people who have finished the eLearning and need a little extra help. Both of our Foundations pay those Soul Healing Disciplers because their expertise is highly sought after and valued.

Our prayer as we wrote this course and book is that thousands and then millions of people will be healed and set free because even in our toughest situations God can redeem ALL things for His good (Romans 8:26-28). We have often seen clients' biggest breakthroughs come after their darkest nights of despair.

Thank you for letting us be your guide in this healing journey for your-self. We pray for you daily that your life will be restored through this book and course.

Many blessings on your healing journey,   Patti and Keren

This course starts (Lesson 1) with *Where Was God?* because until you can answer that question, you will be unable to trust Him with your deepest pain. We then cover the core foundational Lesson 2 on *Understanding Your Body, Soul and Spirit.* It all starts with seeds (trauma/pain) which become roots (your thoughts) and then fruit (emotions and behavior). In this lesson you'll take your understanding and knowledge from your head to your heart for true-life change. Transformational *In Utero Trauma Healing* (Lesson 3) is where your journey begins at the time of conception.

Once your spiritual foundation is set, you'll be *Gaining Freedom from Family Imprints* by address-ing sin patterns from your maternal and paternal families. You may have been drawn to certain sins and never understood why. In Lesson 4 you'll discover why and how to have victory over family strongholds.

You'll break free from the wounds that you have control over, in the next two lessons. Lesson 5, *Breaking Your Inner Vows,* teaches the importance of your own words and the impact they can have on your life. Enjoy newfound freedom by *Breaking Your Inner Vows* and living more freely in Christ. In Lesson 6 you'll *Gain Freedom from Bitter Root Judgments.* You may not realize that it may be your own judgments that prevent others from blessing you. In this les-son you'll release your bitterroot judgments in order to positively change your personal relationships.

The final two lessons deal with wounds that have been caused by others. In Lesson 7, *When Others Curse You Intentionally or Unintentionally,* you'll break curses that have been spoken over you and curses you've spoken over others. In Lesson 8, we address the *Breaking Soul Ties that Bind You,* in a powerful lesson that is sure to address past traumas.

We close out with Lesson 9 *Walking in Freedom* with Holy Spirit inspired tools that will help you walk in victory.

We have two bonus lessons in the back. It is excellent content that you can read on your own. *Who Owns This Problem?* will help you to understand the problems that affect your own inner healing because other peoples' problems cannot be owned or healed by you. You are not their fixer only God is. This is His job not yours.

Understanding *Codependency vs. Interdependency* helps you have healthier relationships and take care of yourself. It enables you to break free from patterns of excessive reliance on others, fostering independence and healthier interpersonal relationships.

At the end of each lesson we'll ask for you to complete your own **Personal Victory** for notes on your healing victories from each lesson. We also provide a **Gratitude Journal** where you can record the positive changes you see and are grateful for in your life.

Acknowledgements

Patti Hathaway: I would like thank Dr. Sandy and Greg Burkett for teaching the Breakthrough Biblical Counseling Training program where I learned these concepts and tools. It transformed my life and marriage. The first book we co-authored as a Bible Study has impacted thousands of people. I'm grateful to hear the many breakthrough stories of God's grace and redemption in healing soul wounds.

A special thanks to my spiritual mentor Pat Masucci who taught the original soul healing Bible Study with me in the Ohio Reformatory for Women. Thank you Pat, for your teaching insights and for sharing your godly wisdom with me. You have courageously spoken many truths in to my life and I am grateful for your mentorship.

Keren Anderson: I would like to thank Jackie Ward for inviting a group of us to go to Zion Christian Fellowship in Powell, Ohio. There I found my purpose and destiny handed to me on a silver platter. I was in a training session to learn Sozo and the tools they use. Father God spoke to me audibly, "I created you for this, Keren."

I was eager to go after learning all I could about this kind of deliverance. I was trained by the Regional Director for Bethel-Redding, Cheryl Kirkham. She is and was a great teacher and mentor to me. I also received the best training with Ann Diffenderfer, Elaine Keith and Lucinda Whitehead. I appreciate the many facets of gentle, kind deliverance. This was a different approach that honored the client and one I fell in love with.

Dedication

We dedicate this book to the best soul healing lead we have ever trained, Anita Penhorwood. She was a great model of motherhood, entrepreneurship and soul tribe leader. In a humanitarian act, she gifted all her beauty shops to women going into their own businesses. Anita's vibrant personality is sorely missed by all who loved her and she's cheering us on in the great cloud of witnesses.

Instructions for Course and Book

Please approach this book in a far different way than you have approached an Inner Healing book before. How can we ask this and what does this mean?

This course and book is to be done from the approach that there is a Living Father God, Jesus and Holy Spirit, the three in One, the Holy Trinity. Throughout the book we capitalize the Holy Trinity as THEM or THEY depending on the context. THEY aren't angry with you. THEY love you unconditionally and want to do this book with you.

Listen to the words we found in Dr. Brian Simmons devotional[1]. "Let Me be your loving Father. I long to teach you what it means to be a son or a daughter of the living God. No matter what your relationship was like with your earthly father, you have a Father in heaven, who has a burning love for you. I cherish you and will give you the fruits of sonship. Let Me teach you the secrets of what it means to be My child. Turn your eyes to Me and know that you have My full attention.

If memories of childhood bring pain and prevent you from knowing Me fully, I will heal that pain and give you a new history in Me. Together we will write a new story of love, patience, encouragement and safety. If you were able to find My love through your earthly father, allow Me to build upon that and give you a new frame of reference. I want you to know that I will always be good, faithful and kind. You can anticipate joy. And you never have to wonder if I'll come through, because you will never again have reason to doubt My love."

> *"If you, imperfect as you are, know how to lovingly take care of your children and give them what's best, how much more ready is your Heavenly Father to give wonderful gifts to those who ask Him?"*
>
> **Matthew 7:11**

If this type of conversation is not your norm, then through this book and a working partnership with Father God, Jesus and Holy Spirit, you will be helped to achieve a closer relationship with this Holy Trinity.

A Few Helpful Instructions:

At the end of each chapter are the answers for the fill-in-the-blanks you will find as part of your journey through this book. You can either fill in the blank when listening to the eLearning or you can pre-fill the blanks prior to watching the eLearning. The page number and answer will always be on the screen to help you.

A little bit of work makes the intake of information so much easier. Much like a little bit of sugar helps the medicine go down better. Our minds digest information the same way as our stomach and taste buds digest what we put into them.

 During the eLearning course, you will see many Personal Assessments and Applications. Most have several lines where you can write your answers that THEY will help to give you. Please pause the video for as long as you need to put your answers in because we will use those assessments and applications at the end of each lesson when we go through the Healing Prayer process. Step by step, line upon line we will break through your strongholds and help you heal your body, soul and spirit.

We work with THEM each step of the way because...

> *"This counsel also comes from Lord YAHWEH, Commander of Angel Armies. For His guidance is unfathomable, and the heavenly wisdom He imparts is magnificent."* [2]
>
> **Isaiah 28:29**

This book is set up in an organized way to be imprinted in your mind the steps to take to heal your soul which are:

1. Your Hiding Place
    a. Find the Lies of the Enemy
    b. Divine Exchange
    c. The Truth
2. Decrees
3. Activation for Change

By the end of the course, you will personally understand how you can walk in victory. You will defeat the enemy in each lesson when you do the work. You will finish with a war chest of tools (our book) filled with healing prayers and a structure you now understand and can use with others. We have a weekly call where you can ask questions and learn more tools from the authors as well as guest speakers.

Understand the Value of His Blood

Jesus shed so much blood even when one drop of His blood would have been enough. Why did He do His crucifixion the way He did? He allowed the free will of mankind to do what it would do to Him. The Holy Trinity will never step on my free will or yours. He knew that His giving of His life force would be purchasing everything needed to give you an Abundant Life here on Earth.

The question becomes this… Jesus, please show me how to give You the value of Your blood back to You. It is very simple:

> *"So let God work His will in you. Yell a loud no to the Devil and watch him make himself scarce. Say a quiet yes to God and He'll be there in no time. Quit dabbling in sin. Purify your inner life. Quit playing the field. Hit bottom, and cry your eyes out. The fun and games are over. Get serious, really serious. Get down on your knees before the Master; it's the only way you'll get on your feet."*
>
> **James 4:8-10** (The Message)

> *"Submit yourselves therefore to God. Resist the devil, and he will flee from you."*
>
> **James 4:7** (KJV)

The answer is to give Him every problem by handing it to Him to fix. In our course, we call this the Divine Exchange. When you give up your free will of wanting it fixed the way you want it fixed, this becomes your resistance against the enemy of your soul. It becomes your shield that wards off attacks. Yes, Jesus defeated the dark kingdom, and His Kingdom became yours. Yet, there are still problems that have to be surrendered to THEM to fix. When you don't surrender each problem, you make a bigger mess of that problem and often it reproduces more problems.

Each time you give THEM a problem and THEY want to solve them all, in THEIR timing, you have just given Jesus some of the value of His blood back to Him.

Why? Because His Blood bought for you, your abundant life, and He wants you to live that abundant life that He bought with His very Life Blood. You have to patiently wait for His timing.

Our prayer is that as you encounter the Lord through the hiding place process, you will heal in His Presence. He will restore you and make all things new. For those who need additional soul healing work after the course, our Foundations have Discipler-Coaches who have gone through this course and the healing process and now they walk alongside those who need additional help. Once you've completed the course, visit your nearest Community Action Center to set up a Discipler Coach relationship with one of our Intake Counselors.

Welcome to **Healing Your Soul!**

 **Resources**

(1) Used with permission from 365 Daily Devotional, *I Hear His Whisper*. Brian Simmons and Gretchen Rodriguez. January 18, Copyright 2019.

(2) All Scripture references are taken from The Passion Translation unless we indicate otherwise.

Where Was God?

I have a pretty simple view of life based on John 10:10. There are two things going on in life:

The enemy of your soul (the devil) comes to steal, kill, and destroy your life.

God comes to give you life more abundantly. And He declares (Jeremiah 29:11) that His plan is to prosper you and not to harm you. He has plans to give you hope and a future.

You have the power to decide which you're going to focus on regardless of what is happening to you at the moment. Will you allow satan to destroy you or God to work all things together for your good? (Romans 8:28).

The most important take-away I got from the year and half we were in marriage counseling after the Harbor Freight melt down was: Don't get mad at my husband. Get mad at the devil who is using him to try and destroy me. Wow! I would've never considered that because I was furious at my husband and I was literally sick and tired of being yelled at.

My focus was on why he was taking his rage out on me all the time? How could I get out? Was it time for me to let go of my marriage? I knew I could live without my spouse because I had Jesus and I knew He was all that I needed. But I knew the cost to our sons would be irrepairable. I was stuck between a rock (my spouse) and a hard place (my beliefs about my marriage).

When the counselor said it was the enemy trying to destroy me, it changed my perspective.

What also really helped me during that difficult season was a sermon by Steve Thompson that my spiritual mentor played for me years ago on *Your Authority in Christ*. This message radically changed my belief system. While initially, I was depressed with the message, it eventually completely changed my life...for the better! And this sermon will help you understand where God was in your difficult times. It may not be what you think...

1. Your Authority in Christ

A subtle and pervasive misunderstanding is prospering in the church. It is woven throughout your understanding of God's plan for your life and affects most if not all of us. It is so commonly held that it is difficult to recognize as a problem. But it is so powerful that in many cases it actually hinders the demonstration of God's kingdom on the earth. This deception is difficult to overcome because it hides within a deep humility and respect for God.

This misunderstanding is the wrong notion that God is __ _____ of everything on the earth. Most if not all Christians, when confronted with difficulty or evil in the earth, will readily quote "Well, God is in control."

2. While this statement is often a humble acknowledgment of God's omnipotence, in many cases it belies a terrible _____ that much of Christianity has been lulled into.

3. Although this may sound like an outrageous and even heretical idea, God is not in control of everything on the earth. While He is undoubtedly and clearly able to enforce His will at any point He

has _____ His dealings on the earth to working through believers. The idea that God is in control of everything on the earth is not only an unbiblical concept-it may be the greatest _____ to God really gaining control of the earth which exists today. The truth is that mankind's free will is in control of what happens on earth, not God.

4. The Earth is Ours

You have a greater calling than most of you realize. You are not just called to make a difference in the earth—you are called to _____ it. Although many Christians may recoil at the boldness and seeming arrogance of that statement, it is truer than you can imagine. You are called by God to rule in the affairs of earth, not to just stand by and watch it fall into further decay. The Psalmist put it this way:

> *"Why would You bother with puny, mortal man or care about human beings? Yet what honor You have given to men, created only a little lower than the Creator – God crowned with glory and magnificence. You have delegated to them rulership over all You have made, with everything under their authority, placing earth itself under the feet of Your image-bearers."*
>
> **Psalm 8:4-6**

> *"The heavens belong to our God; they are His alone, but He has given us the earth and put us in charge"*
>
> **Psalm 115:16**

5. According to the Psalmist, the earth does not belong to God; it belongs to you because God gave it to you. God has crowned you with amazing _____ . Although it may seem outrageous at first glance, the truth is that God has made Himself dependent on you in His dealings in the earth, because He has given you authority in the earth. God will do nothing on the earth, unless He does it through a person. This was God's original plan and it never changed.

6. God-Given Dominion

When God created Adam and Eve, He gave them, male and female, dominion over the earth. God's original intention was that the man and the woman would be His delegated authority, ruling and reigning on the earth.

> *"And God said, Let us make man in our image, after Our likeness: and let them have dominion ... over all the earth, and over every creeping thing that creeps upon the earth"*
>
> **Genesis 1:26** (KJV)

God's design was for the government of earth to be carried out through men and women. You are the crown of God's creation, reflecting His glory and exhibiting His dominion in the earth. In Adam, God invested _____ over the earth. You were forever set as the governing link between God and the earth.

7. Complete Authority

God gave Adam and Eve such complete authority over the earth that they were able to give it _____. By disobeying God and giving in to the temptation of the enemy, Adam transferred their authority over the earth to satan (see Luke 4:4, 2 Corinthians 4:4).

Now mankind had two great problems:

a. Mankind was no longer under the dominion of God; he was now under the dominion of _____ . By submitting themselves to the word of the enemy and becoming obedient to him, Adam and Eve removed themselves from under God's headship and placed themselves and all future offspring under the dominion of satan.

b. In so doing, they also gave their God-given authority over the earth to satan. God did not give satan authority over the earth. Adam and Eve gave it to satan when they submitted themselves to him.

8. A Complete Fall and Complete Restoration

Now mankind needed someone to stand between them and God, to bring them together again. They also needed Someone to stand between them and satan to break the dominion that satan now had over all people. The problem was that there was no man who could affect this redemption on behalf of the people. All people had fallen when Adam and Eve did, so no person was qualified to bring redemption.

To accomplish man's redemption, God sent His Son Jesus as a man, to live as a man completely fulfilling His will because Jesus qualified as our Intercessor—the One who could join us to God again, and who could break satan's headship over us. In Isaiah 53, we find this prophecy of Jesus' redemptive work on man's behalf.

> *"So I, Yahweh, will assign Him a portion among a great multitude, and He will triumph and divide the spoils of victory with His mighty ones— all because He poured out His life-blood to death. He was counted among the worst of sinners, yet He carried sin's burden for many and intercedes for those who are rebels."*
>
> **Isaiah 53:12**

Through His obedience to the Father, the Man Jesus Christ became the Intercessor Who could join men to God. The Scriptures declare Him to be the sole advocate for man toward God. Whereas Adam and Eve had disobeyed God, and in so doing subjected all people to the domination of satan, Jesus Christ walked in complete obedience to His Father, purchasing back men for God with His _____ (see Revelation 5:9).

> *"There is one God and one Mediator who can reconcile God and humanity—the man Christ Jesus."*
>
> **1Timothy 2:5**

Fellowship with God could now be established between God and His people again, through Christ. Not only did Jesus become the way for people to be restored to God, He also became the way that God could once again gain dominion over the earth. The authority that the first Adam had surrendered to the enemy, the last Adam (Jesus Christ) won back (see 1 Corinthians 15).

> [18]*"Then Jesus came close to them and said, "All authority of the universe has been given to Me.[a]*
> [19]*Now wherever you go, make disciples of all nations, baptizing them in the name of the Father, the Son, and the Holy Spirit."*
>
> **Matthew 28:18-19**

Now God once again had a people who could be His authority in the earth. Jesus, having won back authority on earth, could now mediate and rule in the affairs of earth. However, Jesus did **not** stay on the earth to rule it. He ascended to the Father and is seated at His right hand. So who is now responsible to rule and reign in the earth? It's the _____ , which is the body of Christ.

9. Bridging the Gap

This deception that was identified earlier, that God is in control of things on the earth appears as a gracious, humble, and respectful view of God and His sovereignty. In reality, it is a subtle assault against the church fulfilling God's plan for her. When you see evil on the earth and are excused from praying and seeking justice on behalf of others, you have fallen into the enemy's greatest _____ against the church.

God is not in control on the earth; man's free will is. The Scriptures are clear on this point. John writes, *we know that we are God's children and that the whole world lies under the misery and influence of the Evil One.* (1 John 5:19). The evil, chaos and injustice in our world are examples of this. The disease, suffering and hardship which afflict the nations are also evidence that God is not in control of the earth. However Jesus, the firstborn of the new creation, the last Adam, the new Man, has been granted all authority in heaven and on earth. He gladly gives you His authority to help the church do its job on earth.

Here are the two contrasting, but compatible components of our current reality:

- Jesus has been given all authority in both heaven and earth.
- Yet, the whole world is in the power of the evil one.

These two are compatible if you misunderstand the place of believers in God's purpose. Jesus is on the earth through you. He mediates and rules through His body-the church. He can only change things on the earth through you, as you access and utilize the authority He has gained. Your authority is to come into situations on earth because you are part of His body. To the church, He has given, the assignment of subduing powers and principalities (see Ephesians 3:10).

10. God's Sovereignty and Man's Responsibility

God has provided you with all you need in Christ, but He will ____ do your work for you. He has provided the authority over the enemy through His Son, but you (the Bride of Christ) are the body through whom that authority is to be displayed through, here on this earth.

Jesus has empowered His Bride to bring the message of restoration to all people and to break the dominion of satan over society. In reality, it is not God who is _____ the evil to continue, in this earth, the Bride (you) are. It is difficult for this reality to become our springboard into the deeper levels of THEM. It is too easy to not recognize and utilize the authority that He has given you in Christ.

While many of you passively wait on the Lord to move in His sovereign timing, He is actually waiting on you to complete your work. Look at Jesus' position since His ascension.

> *"But when this Priest had offered the one supreme sacrifice for sin for all time He sat down on a throne at the right hand of God, ¹³waiting until all His whispering enemies are subdued and turn into His footstool."*
>
> **Hebrews 10:12-13**

Jesus is waiting for His enemies to be put under His feet. He spoiled powers and principalities, making a public spectacle of them (see Colossians 2:13-15) but you are called to _____ that victory here on the earth. Consider Paul's statement to the church at Rome:

> *"And the God of peace will swiftly pound satan to a pulp under your feet! And the wonderful favor of our Lord Jesus will surround you."*
>
> **Romans 16:20**

God will crush the enemy, but only under **your** feet. He has provided the victory but you must fight the battles, just as God gave the Promised Land to the children of Israel, yet they had to fight to possess it. You must fight to possess that which God has given you in Christ. You must fight for not only what He has given you personally, but what He has given you as an inheritance-the nations (see Psalm 2:7).

This means in your life that you can't wait for God to intervene because He has given you the authority to fight for your Promised Land. It is time to take your authority and stand in it and fight for the life you want with the tools He has given you.

11. Accessing Jesus' Authority

This authority is found in Jesus, and you initially access it through the simplest, weakest way that you could ever imagine- _____ . In this lesson you will be activated to sit with God in your Hiding Place, and invite Jesus there to be with you. God will then move by His Spirit. Whatever you ask, while abiding in God, He will do for you.

> *"⁷But if you live in life-union with Me and if My Words live powerfully within you – then you can ask whatever you desire and it will be done. ⁸When your lives bear abundant fruit, you demonstrate that you are My mature disciples who glorify My Father!"*
>
> **John 15:7-8**

When you decree you are prophetically speaking into the heart of God for your future. You are establishing a prophetic path for your life that you will walk in, with THEM. You will do this over and over in the healing process in this course and through each decision you make on going.

Why would you not continually abide in Jesus, allowing His Words to abide in you and from that position, ask Him for the things that He puts on your heart? Bringing to Him your broken places, your trauma, your greatest disappointments and your fears. He has promised to do whatever you ask, so that His Father will be glorified through the fruit you bear from the place of healing prayer. You cannot exert this authority at your own whim. You exercise it as you abide in Christ and His Words abide in you.

Prayer is not the only work, but it is the first work of the church. Until you have prayed, there is nothing more you can do. After you pray, you must move in obedience, doing what God has shown you to do. Walking out your commitment with fresh love born of the Spirit.

12. The Keys of the Kingdom.

God has given you the keys of the kingdom of heaven. Keys show you have access and _____ . If you take seriously your responsibility and begin to work out your ownership for your life, family, communities and cities, God will allow you to access the authority of Christ over the enemy.

> *"I will give you the keys of heaven's kingdom realm to forbid on earth that which is forbidden in heaven, and to release on earth that which is released in heaven."*
> **Matthew 16:19**

Just as Adam was God's delegated authority on the earth, so you are called to bring into subjection demonic powers and principalities. Adam was called to subdue the earth naturally and to replenish it, using his God-given authority. You are also called to subdue the earth spiritually affecting change in your world through Christ's authority.

As stated, satan gained authority over the earth, not from God, but from man. Since God did not give satan authority over the earth, then satan does not have the authority over you that you believe him to have. You are no longer submitted to him. Jesus has broken satan's _____ over your life. Our Lord has all authority in heaven and on earth, and He is calling you to use that authority to bind the enemy's work and to loose God's kingdom on the earth. You are **not** waiting on Him to move.

So, if you've been waiting on God to take control of your life or rescue you from your struggles, you'll be waiting a long time. He has given you dominion and the authority to bring into subjection demonic powers in your life. And by the way, difficult people are not the devil although they may be used by the enemy to frustrate and get you off track from your destiny. It's your job and God-given right to begin fighting the battle for your life WITH family and not against them. But alas, that will come in other chapters.

13. Where Was God?

So in essence, this explains where was God when there were significant tragedies such as the Rwandan Genocide, 9-11, wrongful deaths, or oil spills, OR everyday pain such as sickness, accidents, or death. I believe that God was with every Christian who died in the towers on 9-11 and I believe that many became believers at the last moment and He received them. But the cabal had free will to do as they wished because satan is still the ruler of this earth.

God is waiting for you to step into your authority. To heal the sick and raise the dead. To do even more than what Jesus did when He was on the earth.

> ¹²*"I tell you this timeless truth: The person who follows Me in faith, believing in Me, will do the same mighty miracles that I do—even greater miracles than these because I go to be with My Father!*
>
> ¹³*For I will do whatever you ask Me to do when you ask Me in My name. And that is how the Son will show what the Father is really like and bring glory to Him.*
>
> ¹⁴*Ask Me anything in My name, and I will do it for you!"*
>
> **John 14: 12-14**

This sermon also helped me to understand why God doesn't intervene in terrible situations such as sexual abuse or molestation of children, or the terrible mistreatment of people in general.

God is omnipresent so He is everywhere but He has given **you** the authority on earth, and largely, the church has missed this and so have you. You haven't stepped up and challenged the status quo. You haven't intervened in the abuse of others.

But what I do know is what the Psalmist says of God:

> *"⁸You've kept track of all my wandering and my weeping. You've stored my many tears in Your bottle—not one will be lost. For they are all recorded in Your book of remembrance.*
>
> ⁹*The very moment I call to You for a Father's help the tide of battle turns and my enemies flee. This one thing I know: God is on my side!"*
>
> **Psalm 56:8-9**

God has promised to redeem all bad things for His good.

It's important for you to know and accept from Romans 8:28 that every detail is woven together for your good. You now come to what is considered one of the most beloved Scripture verses.

Your heart must cling to this precious promise as you navigate by faith through life's journey. For, as much as you may wish it differently, your journey is sometimes painful, difficult and confusing. Yet, you can have an eternal hope in your heart that carries you through, knowing God is weaving every detail (the good and not so good) into a beautiful tapestry. He has a plan...and it's good.

> *"26And in a similar way, the Holy Spirit takes hold of us in our human frailty to empower us in our weakness. For example, at times we don't even know how to pray, or know the best things to ask for. But the Holy Spirit rises up within us to super intercede on our behalf, pleading to God with emotional sighs too deep for words.*
>
> *27God, the searcher of the heart, knows fully our longings, yet He also understands the desires of the Spirit, because the Holy Spirit passionately pleads before God for us, His holy ones, in perfect harmony with God's plan and our destiny.*
>
> *28So we are convinced that every detail of our lives is continually woven together for good, for we are His lovers who have been called to fulfill His designed purpose."*
>
> **Romans 8:26-28**

This is from Dr. Brian Simmons email devotional, ***"Not Guilty"***: We don't judge our life (nor anyone else's life) based on one bad day, one failure, or one difficult season. We may live "one day at a time," but we certainly don't view our lives in a short-sighted, day-by-day way. Rather, we view our lives decade by decade, knowing that God has a wondrous, grand plan that He is working.

Think of Joseph's life, for example. Betrayed, lied about, falsely accused, and imprisoned— not for days, not even for months, but for many years. It was a journey, not an event. And so it is for you and me. Some of the most beautiful words in the Bible are seen in the account of Joseph's heart-rending process.

> *"The Lord was with Joseph"*
>
> **Genesis 39:2 (NIV)**

This is repeated several times in his story. In other words, his story, his history, was formed through intimacy by the faithful love of God. God never failed or forsook Joseph...but that was not how it may have seemed during the process. During those desolate prison years, it appeared as if God had changed His mind about Joseph's destiny, but He hadn't. He was actually faithfully bringing Joseph into his full destiny. It is the same for you and me. Don't lose hope in the desolate moments. Don't despair because the truth is that your journey is not finished. He promised to finish what He started in you, and He surely will.

Growing into Your Answer from God

For Joseph, the day came when his dream was fulfilled. All his brothers were at his feet, and in that beautiful moment, he had no desire to "rub their faces" in their failure. Instead he said these gracious words:

> *"God sent me ahead of you to preserve for you a remnant on earth and to save your lives by a great deliverance. So then, it was not you who sent me here, but God...You intended to harm me, but God intended it for good to accomplish what is now being done, the saving of many lives"*
>
> **Genesis 45:7–8; 50:20 (NIV)**

How could Joseph respond in such a way? Because he fully realized what we must also realize: the powerful truth of Romans 8:28. Everything—the good, the bad, and, yes, even the ugly—will all fit together into God's wonderful, redemptive tapestry of our lives... not just for our good but also for the good of many others.[1]

What you will learn in this course that may radically change your life is how to draw close to the only One Who can transform ashes into beauty and pain and trauma into victory. This journey to a fulfilling life may require you to re-think some of your beliefs. As you do this transformational healing of your soul it will definitely stretch you, cause you to think differently. Most importantly draw you into a relationship with the Lord, it will be life-changing in the very deepest parts of your soul.

He knows you. He's not mad at you. He calls you His beloved. He crowns you with loving kindness and tender mercies. Isn't it time to let down the wall you've built around your heart and let Jesus carry your burdens? By the end of this course, your life will be renewed and you are going to straighten out the crown on your head as the King of King's son or daughter and walk in your authority like the royalty you are.

Hiding Place Activation

In this week's activation you will discover your own personal hiding place. A place where you can meet with Jesus any time you want.

Jesus knows that you sometime have internal conflicts when you come to Him. He never rejects you for that. In fact, His response to a father who cried out and said with tears, *"Lord, I believe; help my unbelief"* (Mark 9:24), was compassion and deliverance for that man's son. That same Jesus longs to have you experience His deep love and healing. Jesus longs to restore wholeness of your soul, spirit and body so that you can know Him and experience the abundant life (John 10:10).

To know the Father is not just to know facts about Him. It is to intimately know Him personally, to experience Him in your emotions, to be able to fully trust and rely on Him in spirit and to have healing in your body, soul, and spirit. When you experience that wholeness, then you can love the Lord with all of who you are (Matt 22:37).

Do you know how God looks at you? In Song of Songs 2 verse 4 it says, *"He looked upon me with His unrelenting love divine."* A person can never look at you with unrelenting love divine but God does. He sees you. He. Loves. You. He sees your pain and He wants to walk alongside you to heal your deepest wound. In fact in verse 6, it says, *"His right hand holds me close. I am to rest in this love."*

The Hebrew name "**Emmanuel**" literally means "**God is with us**". ... When the Israelites came to worship the Creator and **Lord** of all, they sought "**Emmanuel**" as they hoped to experience **God's** presence. Isaiah (7:14)

All through Scripture. the Lord communicates truth by using creative word pictures, such as Isaiah talks about. God gathers the lambs in His arms and carries them close to His heart (Isaiah 40:11). The Psalmist talks about being covered by the wings of God and finding refuge under His feathers (Psalm 91:4). In both cases, the Lord was speaking metaphorically, creating a picture in the reader's mind so that he or she could better comprehend God's protective care

One unique aspect of this soul healing approach is that the Holy Trinity leads the session. While I guide you through the healing prayer words, the Lord directs the session. In Psalm 25:14, God says: *There's a private place reserved for the devoted lovers of Yahweh, where they sit near Him and receive the revelation-secrets of His **promise**.* He creates a Hiding Place where you can connect or be with Him.

A refuge where you know Holy Trinity is there, bringing strength, comfort, peace, insight and healing. This step is foundational in the healing of your soul, because you'll be invited to go back to this Hiding Place of safety with Jesus in each lesson.

The Hiding Place:
* Sit quietly in a comfortable position. Close your eyes the entire time so you're not distracted. Take several deep breaths, letting them out slowly. Again breathe in, breathe out. I use The Passion Translation for all these verses. I'm going to list the verses here for you to read over yourself when you do this on your own.

Psalm 31: 20 *So hide all Your beloved ones in the sheltered, secret hiding place before Your face. Overshadow them by Your glory-presence...*

Tuck them safely away in the tabernacle where You dwell.

Psalm 9:9 *All who are oppressed may come to You as a shelter in the time of trouble, a perfect hiding place.*

Psalm 36:7 *O God, how extravagant is Your cherishing love! All mankind can find a hiding place* under the shadow of *Your wings.*

Psalm 17:8 *Protect them from harm; keep an eye on them like You would a child reflected in the twinkling of Your eye. Yes, hide them within the shelter of Your embrace, under Your outstretched wings.*

Psalm 91 changed to first person. It's important for you to say this out loud because there is power in our words:

When I sit enthroned under the shadow of Shaddai, I am hidden in the strength of God Most High. ^{2} *He's the hope that holds me and the Stronghold to shelter me, the only God for me, and my great confidence.* ^{3} *He will rescue me from every hidden trap of the enemy,* $^{9-10}$ *When I live my life within the shadow of God Most High, Our secret hiding place, I will always be shielded from harm.*

^{14} *For here is what the Lord has spoken to me: "Because you have delighted in Me as My great lover, I will greatly protect you. I will set you in a high place, safe and secure before My face.* ^{15} *I will answer your cry for help every time you pray, and you will find and feel My presence even in your time of pressure and trouble. I will be your glorious Hero and give you a feast.*

 **Pray:** *Holy Spirit, I ask You to take over my soul and purify my imagination. Let my thoughts, be Your thoughts. My creative mind is Your creative mind. I ask You now to show or create within my mind a Hiding Place where You and I can meet.*

When you're ready, invite the Lord to join you in that place. **Say outloud:** *Lord, I want You to join me in my Hiding Place. Come now Lord and show me where You are.*

When you're ready to conclude the activation, simply spend a few moments in thanks and praise to Jesus for being with you.

The Hiding Place exercise may take time to develop as a [spiritual] skill. Many believers, accustomed to a more analytical expression of their Christian walk may have never experienced Jesus in this way.

The idea of giving Holy Spirit access to your "creative imagination" might seem like a foreign concept. It's important that you practice this spiritual exercise every day so you know and experience this intimacy with Jesus at any time. This will be not only a place of peace with Jesus, but it also will be a path into experiencing Jesus in the healing of past traumatic hurts or trauma.

IF you have problems connecting with God in your Hiding Place, please read pages 227-228 in the back of this book that will provide some ideas to help you get there.

Breakthrough Decrees

In preparation for your Breakthrough Decrees, best-selling author Tony Robbins (3) found there are two main approaches to shifting your mind or emotional state: change your physical posture and your focus. _____ creates emotion which changes your thinking. You are body, soul and spirit so action along with speaking out loud activates your body and soul. This will make your spirit cheer you on to victory!

When you consider how Jesus interacted with people, He required them to take a physical action. "Come, follow me," "Get up! Pick up your mat and walk." "Go wash in the pool."

The simple act of engaging in physical activity boosts your heart rate and releases hormones like adrenaline and endorphins. It also triggers neurotransmitters like dopamine and serotonin which enhances your mood. These physical changes solidify that truth thought in your mind and body. And you have a greater possibility of maintaining those transformed thoughts in your life.

These actions could be as simple as standing up. Shaking your fists while shouting your new truth. The hands up victory sign. Point at something or someone and tell them your truth.

Personal Application/Exercise

Personal Activation: Ask THEM, what physical action do you want me to do to activate Your truth in my body and soul?

_____

_____

Now add that truth and action to your list of Breakthrough Decrees for this week.

> *"Death and life are in the power of the tongue and those who love it will eat its fruit."*
>
> **Proverbs 18:21** (NKJV)

When you combine prayers and decrees with actions you become more intentional about the power of your words. In Romans 4:17 TPT it states *"For in God's presence he believed that God can raise the dead and **call into being things that don't even exist yet**."* Decrees are a legal tool to help you align your faith and create a soul full of hope and courage even though you don't see it in the natural yet. These decrees can become weapons to change who you are in Christ.

> *You will also decide and decree a thing, and it will be established for you; And the light [of God's favor] will shine upon your ways."*
>
> **Job 22:28** (AMP)

By definition, a decree is an official order issued by a legal authority. As a believer, you've been given that legal authority. The process of decreeing lays down a prophetic path that you partner with THEM to walk this out in your life. Therefore, you establish the decree(s) out loud on a specific day and year.

At the end of each lesson, you will have a list of Biblical Decrees* that you say out loud to get the lesson concepts deep into your soul. *"Death and life are in the power of the tongue and those who love it will eat its fruit"* (Proverbs 18:21 NKJV).

Breakthrough Decrees (repeat daily)
(activate your words with body action)

1. The past is past. This is a new season and a new day. God in His great mercy, compassion and power, is faithfully bringing me into a glorious future. (Lamentations 3:22-23)

2. God is restoring my life and redeeming all that the devil stole from me for His glory. I know that You can do anything and no plan of Yours can be thwarted. (Genesis 2; Colossians 1:13-14; Job 42:2)

3. My God is the Lord of Breakthrough, and He is breaking through for me and my family. Like a mighty flood He is breaking through every hindrance, delay, interference. He is accelerating me into a new territory and a new level. (2 Samuel 5:20; Isaiah 59:19)

4. God is with me. He is blessing me. That which has been stuck is now unstuck. That which was blocked is now flowing freely. That which was delayed is now accelerated. (Deuteronomy 28:8; Psalm 115:9, 14-15)

5. Nothing of the enemy will be able to stand against me because God is with me. I am strong and courageous, for the Lord is with me wherever I go, and He never fails me nor leaves me! As for me and my house, we will serve the Lord. (Joshua 1:5-7; Joshua 24:15)

6. My truth to replace the lie:_____

    On this day _____, I establish these decrees that are founded in God's Word.

    Signed: _____

Homework This Week

1. Read through the first half of this lesson on *Where was God?*
    Then spend some time in your Hiding Place and ask the Lord
    what questions you have about your authority in Him. You
    can ask any remaining questions during the Q & A Mentoring
    call. This is a crucial concept to understand so you can walk in
    victory in your life.

2. Go to your Hiding Place at least once more. Have an Emmanu-
    el moment with God in Your Hiding Place. Once Jesus is there,
    ask Him: Jesus, what is Your vision for my life?

    Write down what you heard/felt/sensed in Your Personal Notes
    section at the end of this lesson.

3. New Habit: Start your Victory and Gratitude Journal.

Fill-in-the-Blank Answer Guide

1. in control
2. passivity
3. limited hindrance
4. rule
5. authority
6. dominion
7. away   a. satan
8. blood church
9. ploy
10. not   allowing   enforce
11. prayer
12. responsibility   headship
13. Action

Personal Notes

Resources

For more gratitude journal prompts, visit:
https://sheslivingherbestlife.com/gratitude-journal-prompts/

Steve Thompson's article was adapted from *The Morning Star Journal*, Volume 16-The Kingdom, No.3, Kingdom Power. Copyright 2006 MorningStar Publications, Inc.

(1) Used with permission from Dr. Brian Simmons. Not Guilty: Email Devotional Received by email 1/18/2024

(2) Tony Robbins. https://www.tonyrobbins.com/

 **Your Victory Journal**

Write down what victories/wins you experienced this week.

_____

_____

_____

_____

_____

_____

_____

_____

_____

_____

_____

_____

_____

_____

_____

_____

_____

_____

_____

_____

_____

_____

_____

_____

Daily Gratitude Journal

Write down 3 things you are thankful or grateful for each day.

Date:_____ 1. _____

2. _____

3. _____

Date:_____ 1. _____

2. _____

3. _____

Date:_____ 1. _____

2. _____

3. _____

Date:_____ 1. _____

2. _____

3. _____

Date:_____ 1. _____

2. _____

3. _____

Date:_____ 1. _____

2. _____

3. _____

Date:_____ 1. _____

2. _____

3. _____

Date:_____ 1. _____

2. _____

3. _____

Date:_____ 1. _____

2. _____

3. _____

Understanding Your Body, Soul and Spirit

It is crucial to understand the difference between your body, soul, and spirit. In this foundational chapter, you will learn where sin lies so that you can break through your sin patterns and then begin the process of healing your inner wounds (which we will learn in later lessons). This lesson will teach you how to take your understanding and knowledge from your head to your heart for true-life change. God wants you to have victory over your sin by following His pattern for our life.

1. You were created in the _____ of the triune God. Your God is one God, yet He reveals Himself to people in **three** separate yet totally unified ways:
   a. God the Father
   b. God the Son who is Jesus the Christ
   c. God the Holy Spirit.

> *"For there are three that bear record in heaven, the Father, the Son, and the Holy Spirit: and these three are One."*
>
> **I John 5:7** (King James Version)

2. You were also created in a similar manner as **three** distinct yet unified parts that together make up one person.

> *"And God said, Let us make man in Our own image, after Our own likeness."*
>
> **Genesis 1:26** (American Standard Version)
>
> *"See the Word of God is alive! It is at work and is sharper than any double edge sword. It cuts right through to where <u>soul</u> meets <u>spirit</u> and <u>joints meet marrow (body)</u>, and it is quick to judge the inner reflections and the attitudes of the heart. Before God nothing is hidden, but all things are naked and open to the eyes of Him to whom we must render account."*
>
> **Hebrews 4:12-13** (Complete Jewish Bible)

God created you with a _____, a _____, and a _____.

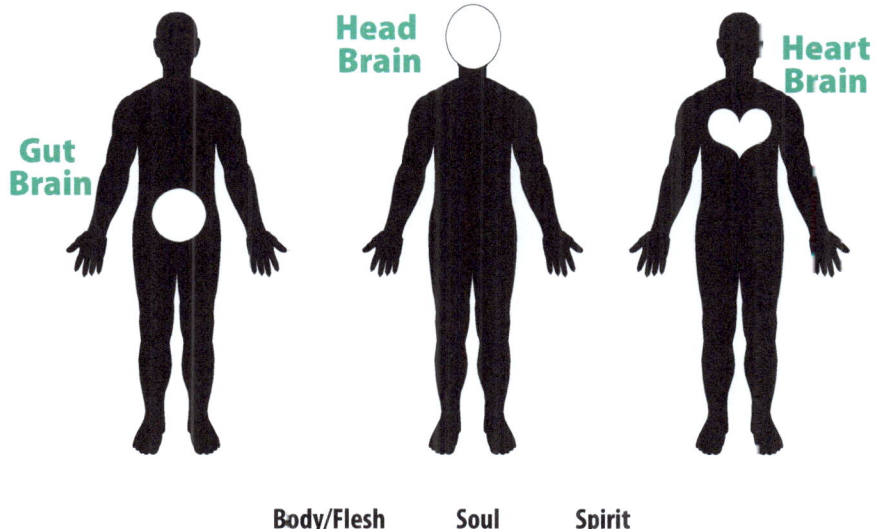

Gut Brain **Head Brain** **Heart Brain**

Body/Flesh   **Soul**   **Spirit**

3. We have _____ brains in our bodies.

This might be surprising but the brain in your head is not the only brain in your body. Neuroscience has shown that your heart and gut are also classed as "brains." It was discovered that you have three brains. The one you most often think about is in your head but you also have one in your heart and one in your gut. Each has complex neural networks that are able to take in information, process it, store it and access it. They each have their own individual functions. (1)

Activation Exercise

You store memories of your hurts and wounds in these three brains. So let's address these emotional memories in your brains through healing prayer. Place one hand over your heart and the other hand above your belly button. The belly button is a place of nurture and is considered the "gut brain."

Visualize the crown of thorns they put on Jesus being put upon your head. Can you see how He encircles the battlefield of your mind with His blood, so you can have victory? We're going to bring His blood to redeem everything in your mind and brains.

Let's invite Holy Trinity into these brains to get them healed.

"Heavenly Father, I ask You to draw the Heavenly plumb line (point to heaven and bring the plumb line down to your body as you speak) *right now in Jesus name, bringing everything in my body into Heaven's perfect alignment for me. I need You* (point up) *to heal my mind* (touch head) *and to create all new neurological pathways in my brains that got messed up by the enemy. Your Word says I have the mind of Christ* (touch head) *so I choose to accept Your perfect mind in the place of my imperfect mind. I command my spirit, soul and body to come into alignment* (point to heaven into your mind) *according to God's perfect design in the name and blood* (touch the nail holes) *of Jesus.*

I command the magnetic polarity to be adjusted and normalized according to Father God's perfect design, in both their north and south polarity (point north and south). *I command any demonic link that has ever been established to be cut off with Your spear* (slash) *that went through Your gut* (touch) *and heart* (touch). *I command that spear to sever* (slash) *all*

demonic links (take that spear and sever it) *that has ever been estab-lished between my* (point to each) *spirit, soul and body in the name of Jesus.*

I ask You, Father God to make Godly connections (point heaven to earth) *between my spirit, soul, body and 3 brains to You in Jesus name. By the blood of Jesus* (touch crucifixion nail holes), *I command every organ, every system of my body, all joints, muscles and nerves* (point to heaven and then touch your body and run it down your entire body) *to come into alignment with Father God's perfect design right now! I ask You, Father God to infuse me with Your divine Life transfu-sion of Your Spirit, Your Truth for all lies, Your Revelation on all wrong thinking patterns and Your total Freedom from the work of the enemy. I receive Your resurrection power of Jesus Christ our Lord into me by the blood of Jesus, that bought all this for me."* Clap because the healing is finished!

Now let's continue on by addressing your whole being with this prayer:

Then pray this out loud:
"I choose to live in this body peacefully, happily and completely, to ful-fill the will God has for my life, which is His purpose that I was created for. Holy Trinity I ask You to fill my inner most being with all of You, in me, in Your proper place upon the thrones of my heart (hand over your heart), *the thrones of my soul, my mind, my will and my emo-tions* (hand on your head) *and the thrones of my body* (touch your body). *I want You* (point up)*to integrate with me* (point to self) *and I want to integrate with You. With all of US becoming ONE* (#1 finger) *together. I need the Fruit of Your spirit that runs through You to run through me. Your Love, Your joy, Your peace, Your long-suffering, Your kindness, Your goodness, Your faithfulness, Your gentleness, and Your self- control, is what I need and want in my life.*

Thank You for accepting me just the way I am at this point in my life. Please process me through my journey here on this earth, until I am ejected from this womb of earth, out of my earth-suit, into my new glo-rious body that You have designed for me. Let me be so integrated with You that Your Fruit of Your Spirit grows naturally from me as it natural-ly grows from You by Your blood Jesus (touch crucifixion nail holes). *As I navigate this journey with You, in spiritual partnership, I now see ACTS 17:28 in a new way. In You, I live and breathe You in with each breath* (take a deep breath) *and in You I have my being. Jesus Your blood bought this for me* (touch crucifixion nail holes). *Thank You* (worship) *for making this possible in Your name and by Your blood* (touch crucifixion nail holes).

What did you experience?

_____

_____

But the fruit of the Spirit is love, joy, peace, forbearance, kindness, goodness, faithfulness, gentleness and self-control. Against such things there is no law. But the fruit produced by the Holy Spirit within you is divine love in all its varied expressions: **joy** *that overflows,* **peace** *that subdues, patience that endures, kindness in action,* **a** *life full of virtue, faith that prevails, gentleness of heart, and strength of spirit. Never set the law above these qualities, for they are meant to be limitless.*

Galatians 5:22-23

4. A Scale of Your Closeness of Your Relationship with THEM

This is the _____Scale. It's like looking through the pane of the window of your heart to see how far AWAY you feel from Father God, Jesus Christ, and Holy Spirit (THEY).

With this in mind-the scale starts as 0 being the greatest distance from you that you feel THEY can be and 10 being the closest to you.

PANE Scale	Far Distance										Closest
Distance from Father God	0	1	2	3	4	5	6	7	8	9	10
Distance from Jesus Christ	0	1	2	3	4	5	6	7	8	9	10
Distance from Holy Spirit	0	1	2	3	4	5	6	7	8	9	10

What number best describes this distance for you with Father God? _____. Why did you use this number?

_____

_____

What number best describes this distance for you with Jesus?_____ Why did you use this number?

_____

_____

What number best describes this distance for you with Holy Spirit? _____ Why did you use this number?

_____

_____

With this same scale let's look at your Identity with the 0 meaning you know nothing about your identity in Father God, Jesus and Holy Spirit and who you are in THEM. A 5 meaning you know somewhat and a 10 meaning you know exactly who you are in THEM.

Identity Scale	Know Nothing								I Know Who I Am		
	0	1	2	3	4	5	6	7	8	9	10

Why did you use this number?

_____

_____

Now let's look at how heavy you feel as to the burden you carry? O means you feel none at all, 5 feels somewhat of a burden and a 10 meaning it can't get any heavier. Please circle one.

Burden Scale	No Burden				Somewhat				Heaviest Burden		
	0	1	2	3	4	5	6	7	8	9	10

Why did you use this number?

_____

_____

What Does My Assessment Mean?

The enemy has covert ways to get your attention off of the Holy Trinity through other human beings that should be the closest to you, yet they may still be hurting you. How do we get this to change?

You may have many _____Father Figures (EFFs) who have messed up your view of Father God. The enemy uses the lens of your EFFs to distort how you see Father God. The way satan does this is to sow _____ into your mind that you believe.

What we believe is what we receive. A lie believed long enough usually becomes an inner vow which we cover in Lesson 5.

Earthly Father Figures/EFF are any authoritarians in your life that had a negative impact on you. Write down the EFFs who apply to you:

_____

_____

In what ways could you be looking at Father God, in this way? Please explain below.

_____

_____

Pause and ask Father God if you have any EFF's that hurt you in any way that you still feel achy/hurt about. Please explain below.

_____

_____

Pause and Ask Father God: Have I transferred any human characteristics from my EFFs onto You? If so, what have I transferred? Please explain below.

_____

_____

5. How Do Trauma/Wounds/Curses Impact Your Soul?
   a. Trauma/wounds/curses lead to negative thoughts because satan _____ to you.
   b. Sin always begins with a _____. You think about something and then you act on it. Your emotions begin with a thought. You cannot feel before you think. *It is your thoughts (your mind) that determine how you feel that influence your choices and what you decide to do (your will).*

ROOTS   **FRUIT**

determine   *influences*

Your Thoughts → **How You Feel** → **What You Do**

(Mind)   (Emotions)   (Will/Choices)

satan lies to you   *impacts your*

➡ **SEED**

(Trauma/Wounds/Curses)   Circumstances

It's important to heal your SEED which comes from trauma, wounds, and curses. You then can change your ROOTS (thoughts) by breaking the power of the lies of satan and renewing your mind with the Truth from God (Romans 12:2). As a result, your FRUIT (how you feel and what you do) will change.

6. How Do You Feed Your Soul? Your soul needs to be fed and nourished with good things, just as a growing child should be fed three balanced meals a day. The absence of these good things can starve and actually _____ your soul.

   a. Some good things that nourish (or lack thereof – starves) your soul include:
   - Affection
   - Beauty
   - Laughter
   - Fellowship and Family
   - Music
   - Cherishing our own person

   b. We all have suffered some degree of woundedness. _____ wounds your soul. The absence of what is _____ also wounds your soul. A wounded soul can affect your walk with Christ and stop you from fulfilling your destiny. When your soul is wounded it can actually imprison your spirit.

c. Your spirit may be ready to move ahead, but your wounded soul can hold you back. You need the _____ _____ of Jesus Christ in order to fulfill your destiny in God's kingdom and to walk in His freedom as overcomers!

7. Today we still deal with the struggle and the consequences of sin. Before you are born again, your spirit is _____ and _____ from God because of sin. Healing the wounds of your life will heal your soul. This process can only begin when you receive Jesus Christ as your personal Savior and Lord.*

When you accept Jesus Christ as your Savior and Lord* your spirit is _____ _____ or regenerated. That is why Christ Jesus said, *"unless one is born again he cannot see the kingdom of God"*. It is your **spirit** that becomes new, **not your soul** and **not your flesh**. Once you are saved you have the ability to change. Without God, you can only struggle to change through self.*

Prayer: *God help me keep my spirit pure and untangled by my flesh and soul. I want to be led by your Spirit and I ask that you daily fill my spirit with your Holy Spirit. In Jesus Name. Amen.*

> *"The sacrifices of God are a broken spirit; a broken and contrite heart—These, O God, You will not despise."*
>
> **Psalm 51:17** (NKJV)

For information on the salvation and in-filling of the Holy Spirit, please read pages 217-224.

8a. We need to address the importance of _____ in the process of healing our soul. In almost every prayer that we have in this book, we include forgiveness.

Whether it's an argument or long-held resentment toward a family member or friend, unresolved conflict can go deeper than you realize—it may be affecting your physical health. It's interesting that 62% of American adults say they need more forgiveness in their personal lives, according to a survey[1]. What is the good news? Even medical studies have shown that the act of forgiveness can reap huge rewards for your health, lowering the risk of heart attack; improving cholesterol levels and sleep; and reducing pain, blood pressure, and levels of anxiety, depression and stress. And research points to an increase in the forgiveness-health connection as you age[2].

"There is an enormous physical burden to being hurt and disappointed," says Karen Swartz, M.D., director of the Mood Disorders Adult Consultation Clinic at The Johns Hopkins Hospital. Chronic anger puts you into a fight-or-flight mode, which results in numerous changes in heart rate, blood pressure and immune response. Those changes increase the risk of depression, heart disease and diabetes, among other conditions. Forgiveness calms stress levels, leading to improved health[2].

 Forgiveness is not just about saying the words. It's an active process in which you make a conscious decision to release your negative feelings towards another and give the pain it caused you to Jesus. You choose by an act of your will to forgive another. It's a divine exchange. Just as you gave Jesus your sin in exchange for His forgiveness (i.e. salvation), in this divine exchange you will forgive the other person (or yourself) and give Jesus your pain. Then ask Jesus what He will give you in exchange for your pain – it's always something better.

There is a great danger when we keep a record or an account (like a ledger) of others' wrong doings in our life. It is one thing by an act of our will, to forgive another person. But when we keep the record or account of that wrong doing in our heart, we really haven't let the offense or wrong doer go. That offense can very quickly become a bitter root judgment (which we will discuss in Lesson 5). With others, this can be a very serious problem when we continue to bring up their past even though you said you forgave them. Trust me, I've been there.

8b. _____ of wrongs are unwritten lists of what people did to you. You believe these records will keep you safe and protected from further harm. That's what the enemy wants you to believe. However, those records do not keep you safe but instead go into an emotional wall that distances your heart from THEM and most other people.

*"Love is not easily angered, it keeps **no record** of wrongs."*
1 Corinthians 13:5b

"Bearing with one another and, if one has a complaint against another, forgiving each other; as the Lord has forgiven you, so you also must forgive."
Colossians 3:13

These Scriptures mean we not only need to forgive them, we need to erase the record of their wrong doing. This doesn't mean we become a doormat to be walked upon. It's important to have God dordained boundaries and hold each other to a standard in marriage. When Jim and I reunited after our nine months of separation, I would NOT allow him to ever raise his voice to me again. No matter how hard it is to forgive or how many times we have to do it, we must remember that forgiveness isn't optional for a Christian.

In the forgiveness prayer you're going to ask Jesus: *Jesus, what records or accounts have I kept about this situation against anyone?* Write down what He shows you.

In the middle of the prayer of forgiveness you will give your records to Jesus: *Jesus, I give You my records/account of* ____<name>____. *What will You do with these records?*

_____

_____

Write down what you see, hear, feel, or sense. It's amazing to see how Jesus handles the records.

Then you'll go through breaking the unforgiveness and offense you have taken on in this situation. Later Jesus will show you what He will give you in exchange for the pain you experienced as well as the wrong doing records you gave Him. This is incredibly powerful when we forgive others as He has forgiven us.

> *"Forget the former things; do not dwell on the past. See, I am doing a new thing! Now it springs up; do you not perceive it? I am making a way in the wilderness and streams in the wasteland."*
>
> **Isaiah 43:18-19**

What wisdom God shares with us in those verses. Giving the records to Jesus can transform any relationship and will build a strong foundation in your life. It's time to let go and let God...

Sample Healing Prayer

Select a person to forgive.

Father God, everything, ____<name>____ *did to me was on Jesus when HE was on the cross. Jesus bought all their sins, just like He bought my sins. By a choice of my free will, I choose to forgive* ____<name>____ *I also give to You the pain this caused* ____<pain>____

_____

Jesus, unlock the prison of my heart (touch your heart) *and escort* _____<name>_____ *out* (pull that person out of your heart).

To my abuser: *I choose to forgive you* ____<name>_____ *and I turn you over* (hand him/her to Jesus) *to Jesus to become the man/woman He created you to be. Goodbye* ____<name>_____ *please go to Jesus with my blessings* (wave good bye).

Jesus, please take any and all records of wrongs (put them in your hands and hold them up to Jesus) *that I have held against* ____<name>_ *and show me what YOU, Jesus, want to do with those records.* Please write what you see/hear/feel.

_____

_____

Jesus, please take me into Your arms and remove all the poison, fiery darts, arrows, daggers and pins (pull them out of your heart, head, back and anywhere else you feel them) *that were inserted into me by the enemy through* ____<name>_____ *. Take the works of the enemy in my mind, will, and emotions, which is my soul, my body and my spirit all away* (touch those parts and brush them all away). *Absorb it completely Jesus and let me feel all of that trauma and drama leave me now* (allow yourself time to feel it leave). *I pray this in Your name and by Your blood* (touch both hands where the nails would have gone through in the crucifixion) *that bought this for me.*

I commit this day to walk out my healing with Jesus' help by His blood and in His powerful name*: Clap!+

_____<signature>_____<date>_____.

*Why do we have you sign and date in each lesson? Signatures hold immense importance in the legal world. They act as a verification method, ensuring that the person signing a document is genuinely themselves. When you sign a contract, your signature serves as a commitment to accept the terms laid out. It becomes a legal obligation. In these lessons, your signature is unique to you, making this healing prayer yours and building trust with THEM that you will walk it out with THEIR help.

+ The Clap signifies that it is over. It is finished in the spiritual realm.

Father God is your best Protector, your best Provider both emotionally and financially, and He will give you, your best Identity in Him. Father God is nothing like human beings, He is Divine.

As part of your homework, please repeat these steps with Jesus and Holy Spirit. This needs to be done from the viewpoint of Jesus regarding your siblings, friends, mates, cousins and co-workers and etc. If you had problems with these people in your life the enemy will use this lens to have your view of Jesus distorted.

Holy Spirit is our Comforter, Nurturer, Teacher and Guide. The enemy uses the lens of your Earthly Mother Figures=EMF's to distort how you see Holy Spirit. Such as: biological mothers, adopted mothers, step mothers, grandmothers, aunts, older sisters that helped raise you, female friends and etc. If you had problems with these EMFs in your life the enemy will use this lens to have your view of Holy Spirit distorted.

In all these areas you have to learn that if there is an aching hurting wound of trauma you have to forgive, give those people over to THEM, release them out of the prison of your heart by forgiving not only with your mouth but from your heart.

Forgiving yourself may be the hardest of all. Understand that people make mistakes and sometimes even intentionally choose the wrong way. But God's love for you is overwhelming and covers a multitude of errors. Stop punishing yourself and thinking you "deserve" this sickness. *He does not treat you as your sins deserve or repay you according to your iniquities. For as high as the heavens are above the earth, so great is His love for those who fear Him; as far as the east is from the west, so far has He removed our transgressions from*

us (Psalm 103:10-12). Substitute yourself in the prayer provided and pray yourself through the forgiveness process.

Bitterness is a lot like a match, it only burns the person holding on to it. When ministering healing prayer, I've found that often unforgiveness blocks a person's healing.

The Bible has a lot to say about forgiveness:

"Get rid of all bitterness, rage and anger, brawling and slander, along with every form of malice. Be kind and compassionate to one another, forgiving each other, just as in Christ God forgave you."

Ephesians 4:31-32

"And when you stand praying, if you hold anything against anyone, forgive them, so that your Father in heaven may forgive you your sins."

Mark 11:25

"And forgive us our debts, as we also have forgiven our debtors. And lead us not into temptation, but deliver us from the evil one. For if you forgive other people when they sin against you, your heavenly Father will also forgive you."

Matthew 6:12-14

> *"Bear with each other and forgive one another if any of you has a grievance against someone. Forgive as the Lord forgave you."*
>
> **Colossians 3:13**

Congratulations! When you forgive someone you are no longer the victim and you can walk in victory.

9. There is one final tool I'd like to share that we will use throughout this book. It's called The _____ Exchange.

Ask Holy Spirit to show you what you need to give up to Him in exchange for something better. Just as you accepted Jesus as your personal Savior when you gave Him your sins in exchange for your salvation.

When it comes to dealing with hurts and trauma you can do a divine exchange by saying: *Jesus I give to you* (list what pain, trauma, negative feeling, situation, etc.) . Put it in your hands and then literally lift it up and give it to Jesus. Put your hands down when you feel you've given it to Him. Then say, *Jesus, what will You give me in exchange for this?* I recommend journaling what you are giving Jesus and what He gave you in exchange for future reference.

Breakthrough Decrees

1. I have the mind of Christ. (1 Corinthians 2:16; Romans 12:2).

2. I am dead to sin and alive to obeying God. I live in obedience to the Word of God because my thoughts, emotions and actions line up with what God says. (Romans 6:11).

3. I walk in ever-increasing health. (Isaiah 53:3-5; Psalms 103:1-3).

4. I set the course of my life with my decrees. (James 3:2-5).

5. God is on my side; therefore I declare that my life cannot be defeated, discouraged, depressed or disappointed. (Romans 8:37; Psalm 91; Philippians 4:13).

6. My truth to replace the lie:_____

   On this day _____, I establish these decrees that are founded in God's Word.

   Signed: _____

* Some declarations used with permission of Steve and Wendy Backlund with IgnitingHope.com

Personal Notes

_____

_____

_____

_____

_____

_____

_____

_____

_____

_____

_____

_____

_____

_____

_____

_____

_____

_____

_____

_____

_____

_____

_____

_____

_____

_____

_____

_____

_____

_____

_____

_____

Homework This Week

1. Join the Weekly Mentoring Call.

2. Say out loud this week's Breakthrough Decrees daily.

3. New Habit: Since words are powerful, I'd like for you to decide in which relationship of yours you need to use different words and/or change your thoughts about that person. Add that new decree to your list of decrees for this week.

4. Go back to pages 36 and 43 on EFFs/EMFs and write out each person that hurt you and make a list of the hurts and forgive them. Matthew 18, says when we don't forgive then we are tormented. Use the Healing Prayer provided.

5. Write in your Victory and Gratitude Journals.

Your Victory Journal

Write down what victories/wins you experienced this week.

_____

_____

_____

_____

_____

_____

_____

_____

_____

_____

_____

_____

_____

_____

_____

_____

_____

_____

_____

_____

_____

_____

_____

_____

_____

_____

_____

_____

_____

_____

 **Daily Gratitude Journal**

Write down 3 things you are thankful or grateful for each day.

Date:_____1. _____
2. _____
3. _____
Date:_____1. _____
2. _____
3. _____
Date:_____1. _____
2. _____
3. _____
Date:_____1. _____
2. _____
3. _____
Date:_____1. _____
2. _____
3. _____
Date:_____1. _____
2. _____
3. _____
Date:_____1. _____
2. _____
3. _____
Date:_____1. _____
2. _____
3. _____
Date:_____1. _____
2. _____
3. _____

1. image
2. body
   soul
   spirit
3. three/3
4. PANE
   Earthly
   lies
5. lies
   thought
6. wound
   b. trauma   good
   c. healing power
7. wounded   separated   born again
8a. forgiveness
8b. Records
9. Divine

Resources

Research Facts about Forgiveness and Health pdf at:
http://releasenow.org/research

(1) http://fetzer.org/resources/fetzer-survey-love-and-forgiveness-american-society

(2) Research from: https://www.hopkinsmedicine.org/health/healthy_aging/healthy_connections/forgiveness-your-health-depends-on-it.

The Art of Forgiving by Lewis Smedes.

A More Excellent Way by Henry Wright.

Feelings Buried Alive Never Die by Karol Truman.

Contend for your Healing by Patti Hathaway

(1) Making Better Decisions Using Your 3 Brains. Lisa da Rocha, B.Sc., MBA, CPCC, PCC. Leadership Labs, Apr 21, 2021. https://ldrleadershiplabs.com/blog/making-better-decisions

(2) Legal Definition of Signature: Understanding the Importance. https://fitterlaw.com/insight/legal-dictionary/define-signature/

Healing In Utero Trauma

Many people have unknown trauma which began in their mother's womb. That trauma then became part of their personality. This lesson and deep inner healing had the most profound impact on my life because I could never figure out why I felt like I didn't belong in my family nor why I was so driven to perform and succeed. There was a deep impact on my marriage from my mother not bonding with me in utero. I didn't have the ability to bond with my beloved and I had an incessant need to perform to be loved. Without God's intervention and healing of our souls, our marriage would have ended.

I have worked with many high performing professionals and executives with similar stories. While we are applauded by colleagues and the world for making great money and achieving success in our work endeavors, often, our personal lives are hurting because we don't have an ability to ever rest. We are driven and we don't know how to stop. When people go through in utero trauma healing they experience similar new understanding and dramatic emotional and physical healing that is both immediate and long-standing. The enemy of your soul tries from the beginning of your conception to steal, kill and destroy your future. This lesson is

---

about to turn that around – to God be the glory!

1. God created each of you wonderfully and uniquely. The shaping of your _____ and _____ began in your mother's womb. What happens to you in the first nine months of your life between conception and birth, molds and shapes your personality, drives and ambitions in important ways.

Psalms 139:13- 16 from the Complete Jewish Bible shares clearly God's intention at the moment the sperm and egg meet.

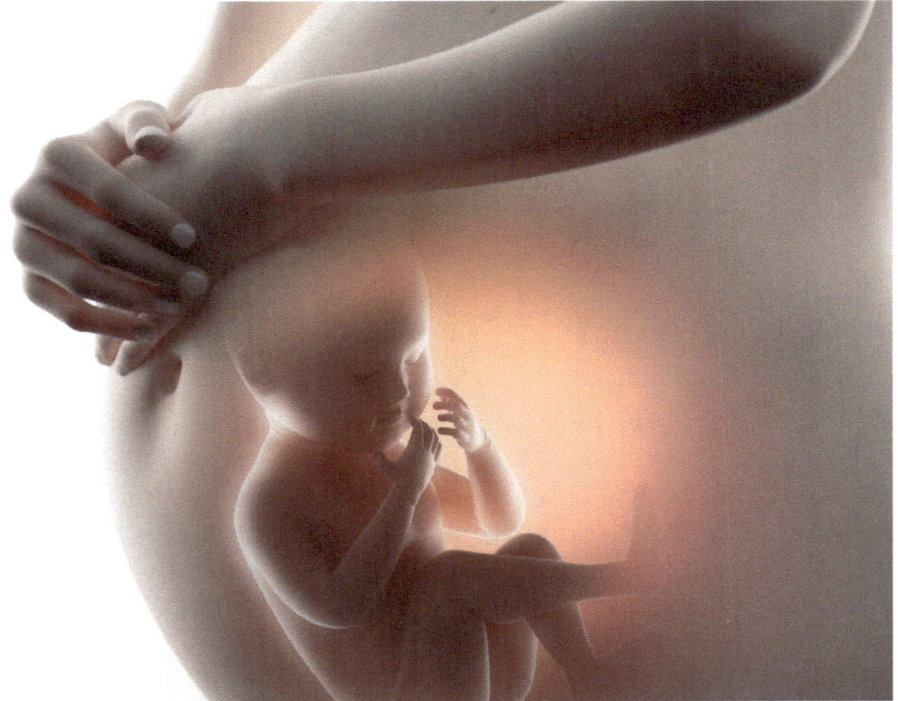

"For You fashioned my inmost being, You knit me together in my mother's womb. I thank You because I am awesomely made, Wonderfully; Your works are wonders I know this very well. My bones were not hidden from You when I was being made in secret, Intricately woven in the depths of the earth. Your eyes could see me as an embryo, But in Your book all my days were already written; My days have been shaped before any of them existed."

2. The Bible teaches that the life of a person begins at conception and science backs up this belief. During the months you were in your mother's womb, your mother was your conduit to the world. Everything that affected her affected you. How your mother viewed the _____ influenced how you

view the world. The beliefs, judgments, and experiences your mother had while carrying you in her womb affected the very core of your _____.

3. Frank Lake, M.D., author of *Mutual Caring*, believes that the first three months of embryonic development are the most _____ part of one's life. Lake's research was based on the scriptures that express that fetal life:

   - Job 33:4 *"The Spirit of God has made me; the breath of the Almighty gives me life."*
   - Psalm 22:9-10 *"Yet You brought me out of the womb; You made me trust in You even at my mother's breast. From birth I was cast upon You; from my mother's womb You have been my God."*
   - Psalm 27:10 *"My father and mother abandoned me. I'm like an orphan! But You took me in and made me Yours."*
   - Luke 1:41 *"At the moment she heard Mary's voice, the baby within Elizabeth's womb jumped and kicked. And suddenly, Elizabeth was filled to overflowing with the Holy Spirit!"*
   - Luke 1:44 *"As soon as the sound of your greeting reached my ears, the baby in my womb leaped for joy."*
   - Eph. 2:10 *"We have become His poetry, a re-created people that will fulfill the destiny He has given each of us, for we are joined to Jesus, the Anointed One. Even before we were born, God planned in advance our destiny and the good works we would do to fulfill it!"*

4. Trauma may begin as early as _____. If the sexual act in which a baby is conceived is hostile, fearful, ambivalent or just for a good time with no commitment on the part of the adults, both the egg and the sperm carry that cellular imprint of conception (*Imprint for Life* by Leah LaGoy).

5. Life in the _____ is remembered. The moment you are conceived you begin to store up treasures and/or traumas in your heart. Those treasures/traumas are made up of the attitudes, judgments (inner vows, bitter root judgments) and expectations you hold.

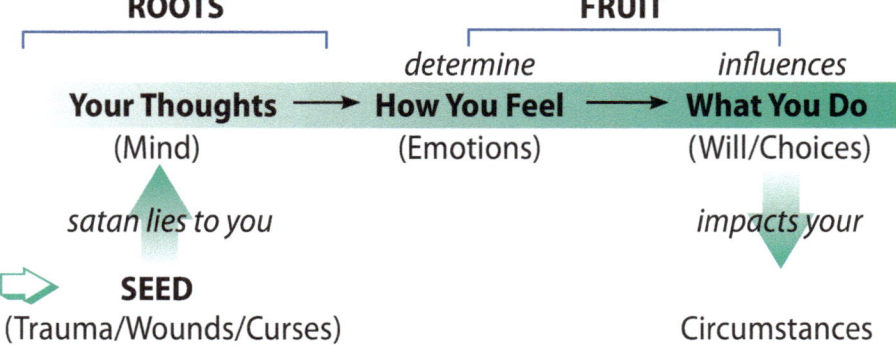

ROOTS		FRUIT	
		determine	*influences*
Your Thoughts →		**How You Feel** →	**What You Do**
(Mind)		(Emotions)	(Will/Choices)

satan lies to you　　　　　　　　　　　　　*impacts your*

⇨ **SEED**

(Trauma/Wounds/Curses)　　　　　　　　Circumstances

This graph makes it clear that your soul (your mind, emotions, and will/choices) needs to be healed and then trained to carry God's thoughts, feelings, and desires. Once healed, you will begin to speak life instead of death over your life.

Many people have trauma they don't even remember. By uncovering where your pain actually began, deep inner healing paves the way for you to not only understand but to heal your deepest pain and physical disease.

Medical Science has discovered this. They know that buried feelings alive, never die. Buried feelings result in physical illness. For example, fibromyalgia and chronic fatigue syndrome are indicators of in utero trauma before you were even born. Hurt and disappointment is linked to changes in your blood pressure, heart rate and immune response. Those changes increase the risk of depression, heart disease and diabetes.

So healing your soul can lead not only to greater happiness and fulfilment in your life but can also heal your body and mind.

This is why I've added a physical dis-ease segment to our healing prayer. Dis-ease refers to physical, emotional, and mental sickness. I've seen many physical, emotional and mental healing miracles from healing one's soul. Be expectant!

- *Psalm 109:22 states "I'm so broken, needy and hurting. My heart is pierced through and I'm so wounded."* A person who has been deeply wounded in utero will express that woundedness as a child, adolescent and adult.

6. A baby growing inside the womb is just like the rest of us, and can experience a whole range of _____ even before entering this world. Some of these experiences may include:

   a. Failed Abortion - post-traumatic stress disorder; nightmares that might be in utero memories are:
   - "...it seems that most of the time they are about loved ones getting hurt or killed.."
   - "...If you think about it all my dreams have a recurring theme of saving myself which involves a lot of aggression, running, violence, getting help, defending myself and overcoming obstacles..."
   - "...I often dream about people dying, and in my dreams everyone else is nonchalant about it, yet I am terribly upset and wake up this way..."
   - "...I have dreamed about being stabbed with a knife more than once..."
   - "...I dream I am drowning..."

   b. Siblings of an abortion and/or miscarriage may experience loss or trauma.

   c. Adoption - Adults who have been adopted may experience emotions such as anxiety, rejection, or abandonment. Other symptoms of a child given up for adoption may be:

   - Death wish and performance orientation
   - Feelings of not belonging, being a burden, loneliness
   - Fear of rejection may cause the child to need too much love or reject love altogether
   - Pathological lying can occur due to the child being lied to either in the womb or during the formative years
   - Kleptomania – the unborn judges that what was rightfully theirs was stolen from them

- Identity crisis may occur and exhibit fruit of trying to be everything to everyone because they fear rejection
- Resentment, defensiveness, anger, rebellion

d. If you experienced famine in utero, you are more prone as an adult to experience severe problems with being
_____.

e. Confusion about your _____ _____. Outwardly you may express your sex/gender but inwardly you may feel confused.

- The child that is identified as an "it" in the womb may feel like an "it" outside the womb.
- The child in the womb who knows that mom or dad wanted a child of the opposite sex experiences rejection and abandonment even before birth. As adults they may experience confusion concerning their sexual orientation.

7. In the 1960s scientists discovered a post-birth system of communication between the mother and child called _____.

a. The womb environment has the ability to disrupt the formation of any stable _____ which can carry over into adolescence and adulthood, making trust and intimacy difficult to obtain.

b. Researchers discovered the most important factor in the unborn child's development is the mother's _____ consistency.

- One of the more harmful circumstances for an unborn child is when the _____ is absent, abusive or neglectful. An equally vital factor in the prenatal child's wellbeing is the father's commitment to the marriage.
- If a mother experiences a significant _____ in her life that causes major distractions, she may withdraw her love and support from her unborn child. This loss may plunge the child into depression.

8. A _____ birth can contribute to traumatic experiences that may lead to emotional or spiritual issues in later life. Some studies are revealing that fibromyalgia and the chronic fatigue syndrome have their origins in severe traumatic births.

9. The attitudes and behavior of a person who is _____ in utero can be summed up in the message found in Job 32:8 (Amplified Bible) *"But there is (a vital force) a spirit (of intelligence) in man, and the breath of the Almighty gives men understanding."* The woundedness you suffered is remembered in your spirit from your subconscious memories. Praise God - those memories can be healed through transformational healing prayer.

Testimony of Offender Heather Speakman, age 44 Testimony:

I sat in a chair closing my eyes taking myself back to the moments in my mother's womb. Feelings of rejection, abandonment, and a very dark sadness was all around me. I didn't want to come out. I wanted to stay in the dark. Patti asked me if I sensed Jesus was there? I didn't at first but then it started getting brighter and brighter. I had an overwhelming feeling that I need to get to that Light. I needed to get out. I wanted to be born. I felt purpose in my life for the first time. I felt love. My In Utero healing has revealed many deep wounds that I continue to take to Jesus to get to the root of it.

Since my In Utero healing I've been able to share this teaching with other ladies like myself. Being reborn with purpose has changed my whole life. I always felt I lacked identity even while being a believer. I always heard you're a new creature in Christ. Literally in those moments of In Utero healing that divine exchange took place; from spiritual death to spiritual life. I am a new creature through Christ Jesus. I have been reborn.

I am truly blessed to have been taught this teaching. My life is forever changed and I share this teaching with my family and others. I know I have purpose and identity which are the elements of an abundant life.

PATTERNS AS RELATED TO IN-UTERO CONDITIONS

THE CONDITION IN-UTERO	COMMONLY OBSERVED PATTERNS OF ATTITUDE AND BEHAVIOR AFTER BIRTH
A child not wanted	Striving, performance orientation, trying to earn the right to be, inordinate desire to please (or the opposite, rejecting before they are rejected), tension, apologizing, anger, wishing death, frequent illness, problems with bonding, refusing affection (or having insatiable desire for same), never feels heard
A child conceived out of wedlock	Having a deep sense of shame, lack of belonging, feels different than others, lack of identity, struggles with relationship with Christ
The parents face a bad time financially	Believing "I am a burden," never asks for anything, becomes a financial miser

THE CONDITION IN-UTERO	COMMONLY OBSERVED PATTERNS OF ATTITUDE AND BEHAVIOR AFTER BIRTH
The parents are too young, not ready, bad timing	Believing "I am an intrusion," feels rejected, confused and feels like they live in the wrong time of life
The mother has poor health	Guilt for being: child may take emotional responsibility for mother
Rough pregnancy	Rejected, ignored, responsible for any pain mother experiences, expresses they feel they are "bad"
A child in utero being what one or both parents consider to be the wrong sex	Death wish. Sexual identification problems, sometimes one of the causes of homosexuality; striving to please to be what parents' want, futility, having a defeatist attitude: *"I was wrong from the beginning," "No matter what I do it will be wrong"* Rebellion-Why should I even try.
The child follows other conceptions that were lost	Being over-serious, over achieving, striving, trying to make up for the loss, anger at being a "replacement," not getting to be "me," struggles leaving home
Mother has a fear of delivery	Fear, insecurity, fear of birth; may choose in the womb not to be born, fear of doctors and hospitals
Fighting in the home	Nervous, fear, jumpiness, anxiety, panic attacks, parental inversion, responsible for others emotions, fear of being born, choosing never to grow up.
Father dies or leaves, father in service, prison, or works away from home more than being at home	Guilt, self-blame, bitter root expectation to be abandoned, inordinate hunger to find things to fill inner void, having a death wish, depression, anxiety, trouble bonding to men
Mother loses a loved one and is consumed with grief	Deep sadness, depression, having a death wish, fear of death, loneliness, imagining *"no support for me; I will have to depend on myself"*
Father unfaithful	Lack of trust toward men, lack of bonding toward men, vow to never become a man, bitter roots toward men
Unwholesome sexual relationship between father and mother	Aversion to sex, fear of male organ, sexual addictions, inability to climax or have intercourse

THE CONDITION IN-UTERO	COMMONLY OBSERVED PATTERNS OF ATTITUDE AND BEHAVIOR AFTER BIRTH
Toxemia	Fear of water, suffocating, at times feels like they are drowning
Mother does not eat properly	Fear of starving, food addictions, anger
Mother does not recognize pregnancy	Rejection, abandonment, believes they are invisible
Mother a heavy smoker	Predisposition to severe anxiety, fear of suffocating
Mother consumes much caffeine	Baby likely to have poor muscle tone and low activity level
Father physically abusive	Hatred toward men, fear of men, anxiety, takes responsibility they are the cause of abusive situations and they are "bad"
Child conceived through artificial insemination into a women who will carry the child but will not continue to mother the child after birth	Rejection, confusion, identity crisis, inability to trust or to bond
One parent practices homosexuality	Hatred toward sexuality, confusion of gender, protective of other parent, guilt, shame, inability to bond, doesn't want to be noticed

Testimony of Sharon Young, prison inmate for 32 years

When I heard the teaching on In Utero Trauma, I admit I was a bit skeptical about going back into the womb. It sounded kind of strange but I figured I trusted these women—if anything went wrong, they could pray me out of it.

I closed my eyes and said, "I'm open Lord if this is something you want for me." I was led to go back to my mother's womb and I did! I thought— I've done snapped because I became a fat little baby just swimming in my mother's womb. I felt everything.

I know that my parents didn't care and they thought I was stupid. I heard those lies even in the womb. They didn't want me. But it's okay that they didn't want me because I felt safe in the womb. I innately knew Jesus loved me because He was there in the womb with me.

When I was ready to be born, I saw a little hole like a pencil end. I swam out. I wanted to be born! I was full of joy because Jesus loves me. I was safe in Him! I said "let's go – let's play!" I cried tears of joy. I saw the light and I was born into Jesus' arms. He really loves me! It was the most profound experience I have ever had.

Two weeks prior to this transformational healing prayer experience. I had a dream that I was holding a fat little baby. I was looking down at this baby. Initially, I didn't know if I was blessing this baby or telling it good-bye or what? Then I realized that I was crying tears of joy. I told my sister about my dream and told her that I had no idea who that baby was or why I was holding it. Very strange. When I went through the In Utero healing prayer, I realized that I was holding myself in that dream. Because I recognized that I was that same fat little baby from my dream two weeks earlier. I actually felt God's love for the first time in my life.

 ## Hiding Place Activation

Sit quietly in a comfortable position. Close your eyes the entire time in a posture of prayer. Remember there will be a lot of quiet time during this activation so just relax in His Presence.

Take several deep breaths, letting them out slowly. Again breathe in, breathe out.

Here are some verses related to your in utero experience to read out loud:

Job 33:4 *The Spirit of God has made me; the breath of the Almighty gives me life.*

Ephesians 2:10 *We have become His poetry a re-created people that will fulfill the destiny He has given each of us, for we are joined to Jesus, the Anointed One. Even before we were born, God planned in advance our destiny* and the good works[j] we would do *to fulfill it!*

Job 32:8 *"But there is (a vital force) a spirit (of intelligence) in man, and the breath of the Almighty gives men understanding."*

First, you're going to pray Psalm 31: 20 over yourself:

²⁰ *So hide me Your beloved one in the sheltered, secret hiding place before Your face. Overshadow me by Your glory-presence…Tuck me safely away in the tabernacle where You dwell. Lord, I want You to take me back to our hiding place now.* Go back with Him to your hiding place. Then rest in His Presence and love for as long as you like.

Praying Scripture Prior to In Utero Healing

Pray from Psalm 139:23-24 TPT. Say out loud: *"God, I invite Your searching gaze into my heart. Examine me through and through; find out everything that may be hidden within me. Put me to the test and sift through all my anxious cares. See if there is any path of pain I'm walking on, and lead me back to Your glorious, everlasting ways — the path that brings me back to You."*

Hebrews 13: 8 *"Jesus Christ is the same yesterday, today and forever."*

Now, we're going to invite Holy Spirit to bring you back into your mother's womb:

1. **Seeker:** *Holy Spirit, I invite You to bring me back to my mother's womb. I trust You in this healing process to reveal to me what happened there.*

2. Tell us when you are there.

3. What do you see/sense?
   How do you feel?
   What pain is there?
   Are you ready to give that pain to Jesus?

_____

_____

_____

4. What records or accounts have I been holding on to against my parents?

_____

_____

_____

Seeker: *I give all this pain* _____ (put in your hands and lift up to Jesus. Put your hands down when you feel you've given it all to Him) *to You Jesus. I also give to You all records* _____ *I've held against my parents. I choose by an act of my will to forgive my mom and dad for the pain they caused me. Jesus, what will You do with those records?*

_____

_____

_____

Write what you hear, see, feel.

Ask Jesus what He will give you in exchange for your pain and your records. Say: *Jesus, thank You for receiving all my pain and records of wrong doings. What will You give me in exchange for my pain and records?* Write what you receive.

5. What emotions do you feel from your parents? **Seeker ask:** *Holy Spirit, please reveal to me what emotions I felt from my parents when I was in my mother's womb that have wounded me.*

_____

_____

_____

In Jesus Christ's name, I break the power of _____(emotions)_____ *which I experienced in the womb. I cancel the assignment of those feelings/ words. I forgive my mother/father and release them to You Jesus to have Your perfect will and way in their lives. I decree all that has been taken by the enemy be restored to me in the name and blood of Jesus Christ.*

Father, in the name of the Lord Jesus Christ, I speak to the inner spirit of this person that their life is not a mistake. You have called this child into being at the right time and the right place. You have known this child from the very beginning. Father, You have never left nor forsaken this child.

6. **Seeker ask:** *Holy Spirit, please reveal to me what lies I believed in the womb.*

_____

_____

_____

Holy Spirit, what is Your Truth for me to counter/break that lie?

_____

_____

_____

Breaking Lies Prayer

In the name of Jesus Christ I confess that I have believed the lie that
_____(lie)_____ . *I make the choice to forgive* _____(name)_____
*who caused me to believe this lie. I ask you, Jesus, to forgive me
for believing this lie. I break the power of this lie that* _____(lie)_____
*in the name of Jesus Christ and I sever it with the Sword of the Spirit.
What is the Truth from Your Word in exchange for that lie?* _____
*I turn my back on this lie and choose to believe_____(the Truth from God's
Word)_____ and I can walk that out in Jesus Christ.*

7. <If Lack Father/Mother Love:> Father in the name of Jesus Christ Your word said that You are the Father and Mother to the orphans. This child of Yours is void of the love of the Father (Mother). I ask the Holy Spirit to come and fill the void of the Father's (Mother's) love. Fill _____(name)_____'s core that has been empty with Your perfect love.

8. **Seeker ask:** *Holy Spirit, show me if I am suffering from any physical, emotional or mental disease due to in utero trauma?*

_____

_____

_____

Physical Healing Prayer

In Jesus Christ's name, I command complete healing and restoration over my body, soul and spirit and specifically the healing of____(disease)_____ caused by in utero trauma. By Your stripes I am healed. Thank you Jesus.

9. Are you ready to be born into the arms of Jesus? **<u>Seeker:</u>** *Jesus, I know that You knit me together in my mother's womb. That You are the same yesterday, today and forever. So, I invite You to hold me as I am born. I am ready...*

10. Can you describe what is happening?
    What is Jesus doing?
    What is He saying to you?
    How are you feeling?

11. Blessing Prayer*: I pray that the eyes of your heart,
    _____(seeker)_____, may be enlightened so that you may know the hope of His calling, the riches of the glory of His inheritance in the saints, and the surpassing greatness of His power toward you. May God grant you, _____(seeker)_____, according to His riches and glory, to be strengthened with power through His Holy Spirit in the inner man. We seal all these prayers with oil in the name of the Father, Son, and Holy Spirit. Amen.
    * Additional Father and Mother Blessing Prayers on pages 73-77.

Breakthrough Decrees (repeat daily)
(activate your words with body action)

1. I am fearfully and wonderfully made (Psalm 139:14).

2. I am God's workmanship, created in Christ Jesus to do good works, which God has prepared in advance for me to do (Ephesians 2:10).

3. I am a man/woman created in God's image.
    (Genesis 1:27).

4. All that has been stolen from me and my life will be redeemed for His glory. (Isaiah 59:15-16; Colossians 1:13).

5. Through Jesus I am 100% loved and worthy to receive all of God's blessings. (Galatians 3:1-5).

6. My truth to replace the lie:_____

    On this day _____, I establish these decrees that are founded in God's Word.

    Signed: _____

* Some declarations used with permission of Steve and Wendy Backlund with IgnitingHope.com

Homework This Week

1. Say out loud this week's Breakthrough Decrees daily. *This helps to transform your mind and perceptions.*

2. New Habit: Find a really good friend or family member to share with what your In Utero trauma was and how it impacted your life, the Truth that you received from Jesus, and what steps you are taking to walk in victory. Share one way they can support you in your healing journey in this area. Pray together over your traumas.

3. Write in your Victory Gratitude Journal daily.

4. Share one of your victories or gratitudes on your personal Facebook page (if you have one). Perhaps that will encourage others to share what they are thankful for.

Your Victory Journal

Write down what victories/wins you experienced this week.

_____

_____

_____

_____

_____

_____

_____

_____

_____

_____

_____

_____

_____

_____

_____

_____

_____

_____

_____

_____

_____

_____

_____

_____

_____

_____

_____

Daily Gratitude Journal

Write down 3 things you are thankful or grateful for each day.

Date:_____1. _____

2. _____

3. _____

Date:_____1. _____

2. _____

3. _____

Date:_____1. _____

2. _____

3. _____

Date:_____1. _____

2. _____

3. _____

Date:_____1. _____

2. _____

3. _____

Date:_____1. _____

2. _____

3. _____

Date:_____1. _____

2. _____

3. _____

Date:_____1. _____

2. _____

3. _____

Date:_____1. _____

2. _____

3. _____

Date:_____1. _____

2. _____

3. _____

 **Fill-in-the-Blank Answer Guide**

1. mind
   personality
2. world
   soul
3. significant
4. conception
5. womb
6. emotions
   d. overweight
   e. sexual orientation
7. bonding
   a. attachment
   b. emotional
      • father
      • loss
8. traumatic
9. wounded

Suggested Reading Material for Further Studies:

The Secret Life of the Unborn Child, Thomas Verny

Healing the Wounded Spirit, John and Paula Sandford

Restoring the Christian Soul, Leanne Payne

Mutual Caring: A Manual of Depth Pastoral Care, Frank Lake

Imprints, Life Long Effects of the Birth Experience, Dr. Arthur Janov

Fear Itself: The Origin and Nature of the Powerful Emotion that Shapes Our Lives and Our World, Rush W. Dozier

Deeply Damaged: An Explanation for the Profound Problems Arising from Aborting Babies and Abusing Children, Dr. Philip G. Ney

Father Forgiveness Blessing Prayer

May I have your permission to speak to you as your father?

Let these be like the words that your father would have spoken to you, if he could have separated from his wounds and if he could have received the love and mercy of the true Father and had His heart to share with you. Let it help release your father from any bitterness you may have toward him and restore a true image into your heart of what your Heavenly Father is really like.

I ask your forgiveness for the things that I have done that have hurt you... Please forgive me... for failing to accept and affirm you
- For not showing you respect for your uniqueness.
- For not giving you freedom to form and express your own opinions.
- For not making you feel that you were the boy/girl I wanted.
- For not giving you the affection and acceptance you needed.
- For not telling you "I love you" and hugging you regularly.
- Will you forgive me?

Please forgive me... for neglecting my responsibilities
- For not keeping my word or my promises to you.
- For not apologizing to you and admitting when I was wrong.
- For not protecting you and making you feel safe.
- For not providing for you financially.
Will you forgive me?

Please forgive me... for abandoning you
- For not giving you my time and attention.
- For not being at your sports games and special events.
- For my silence toward you.
- For abandoning you emotionally and physically.
- For not quitting my addictions for your sake.
Will you forgive me?

Please forgive me... for verbal and physical abuse
- For not building you up, encouraging you and believing in you.

- For embarrassing you in front of others.
- For yelling at you and cursing you in my anger.
- For disciplining you with harshness—making you fear me.
- For physically or sexually abusing you.

Will you forgive me?

Please forgive me… for failing as a husband to your mother
- For not loving your mother.
- For not showing you a man's true responsibilities in the home.
- For not marrying your mother before you were conceived.
- For the times of physical and verbal abuse of her you saw and heard.
- For divorcing your mom and abandoning you.
- Can you forgive me for dying?

Will you forgive me?

Please forgive me… for being a poor spiritual leader; poor role model
- For not being a godly father, for not praying for you or with you.
- For not taking you to church and teaching you about the Lord.
- For not taking a stand for what is right.
- For not modeling for you a healthy picture of the true Father.

Will you forgive me?

I ask your forgiveness for all the ways I was not there for you when you needed me.

Now let's walk through the PRAYER TO FORGIVE YOUR FATHER.

Dear Heavenly Father, in the name of Jesus, I purpose and choose by an act of my will to forgive (open your hands) *my father for all the ways that he failed me or hurt me. I repent for agreeing with the enemy in bitterness about my father. I renounce those things in my life.* Stand up and shake off all that bitterness. *Now, in the name of Jesus I receive Your forgiveness of me and I choose to forgive myself and to fully accept myself* (hug self) *as the child of the father You gave me. Holy Spirit please come… heal my broken heart* (hug self) *and show me and tell me Your truth* (point up)…

I commit (clasp hands) *this day to walk out my healing with Jesus' help by His blood* (touch crucifixion nail holes) *and in His* (point up) *powerful name:* Clap!

_____ \<signature\>_____ \<date\>_____ .

Now I want to give you your FATHER'S BLESSING

Please receive this as if these were the words your father would speak to you if he could be free to receive the heavenly Father's love for you.

- I bless you my precious child. You are so loved—specially created by God, unique and perfect. I am so proud of you. I speak life into you.
- I bless all the relationships of your life that you may grow in friendship and intimacy with your Heavenly Father, with your Lord and Savior Jesus Christ, with the Holy Spirit, and with all your friends and family members.
- I bless your ability to be strong in the Lord and in the power of His might, that you may be a mighty spiritual warrior serving the purposes of God in your generation.
- I bless you and release you into the gifts God has given you to fulfill His plan for you. I love you.

Used with permission of Reverend Annie Arakelian, Clinical Christian Counselor and Board Certified Life Coach. http://lightofthecomforter.org/prayer-for-forgivenesshealingblessing_father-child/

Mother Forgiveness Blessing Prayer

May I have your permission to speak to you as your mother?

Let these be like the words that your mother would have spoken to you, if she could have separated from her wounds and if she could have received the love and mercy of the true Father and had His heart to share with you. Let it help you release your mother from any bitterness you may have toward her and restore a true image into your heart of what your Heavenly Father is really like.

I ask your forgiveness for the things that I have done that have hurt you…

Please forgive me… for failing to accept and affirm you
- For not telling you how precious you were to me.
- For not making you feel that you were the boy/girl I wanted.
- For not giving you the affection and acceptance you needed.
- For giving you up for adoption or for conceiving you out of wedlock.

- It's not your fault. You were not a mistake.

Will you forgive me?

Please forgive me... for poor parenting
- For not letting you enjoy being a child.
- For not protecting you from all the fussing and fighting in our home.
- For not believing you or protecting you from your father's abuse.
- For telling you it was your fault. It was not your fault.

Will you forgive me?

Please forgive me... for taking my emotions out on you
- For telling you that you'd never amount to anything.
- For the anger and frustration I took out on you.
- For saying words that devalued you and shamed you.
- For not giving you freedom to form and express your own opinions.

Will you forgive me?

Please forgive me... for failing to nurture you
- For not showing you unconditional love.
- For not holding you when you were hurt.
- For not taking the time to meet your needs.
- For not spending time with you because I was always busy.
- For not quitting my addictions for your sake.

Will you forgive me?

Please forgive me... for smothering you
- For controlling you and making you do things my way.
- For getting angry if you tried to express your independence.
- For trying to control your every action.
- For manipulating you with guilt and threatened rejection.

Will you forgive me?

Please forgive me... for not being a godly role model
- For not modeling what a godly wife and mother should be.
- For not taking you to church or teaching you to pray.
- For divorcing your father.
- Can you forgive me for dying?

Will you forgive me?

I ask your forgiveness for all the ways I was not there for you when you needed me.

Prayer to Forgive Your Mother (for the Child)*

Dear Heavenly Father, in the name of Jesus I purpose and choose by an act of my will to forgive (open your hands) *my mother for all the ways she failed me or hurt me. I repent for agreeing with the enemy in bitterness about my mother. I renounce those things in my life.* Stand up and shake off all that bitterness. *Now, in the name of Jesus, I receive Your forgiveness of me and I choose to forgive myself and to fully accept myself* (hug self) *as the child of the mother You gave me. Holy Spirit please come heal my broken heart* (hug self) *and show me and tell me Your truth* (point up)......

I commit (clasp hands) *this day to walk out my healing with Jesus' help by His blood* (touch crucifixion nail holes) *and in His* (point up) *powerful name*: Clap!

_____.
<date>

Mother's Blessing

Please receive this as if these were the words your mother would speak to you if she could be free to receive the heavenly Father's love for you.

- I bless you my precious child. You are so loved—specially created by God, unique and perfect. I am so proud of you. I speak life into you.
- I bless your heart that your spouse, friends and children can safely trust in it, that you will have a grateful heart and be thankful for all you have been given.
- I bless your awe and reverence of the Holy Trinity so that you may follow His commandments, walk in His ways and desire to have order and balance in your life.
- Before you were born God loved you and I love you. I honor you. I praise God for you. I bless you now and forever.

Used with permission of Reverend Annie Arakelian, Clinical Christian Counselor and Board Certified Life Coach From: http://thelightofthecomforter.com/2016/prayer-for-forgivenesshealingblessing_mother-child/

Personal Notes

_____

_____

_____

_____

_____

_____

_____

_____

_____

_____

_____

_____

_____

_____

_____

_____

_____

_____

_____

_____

_____

_____

_____

_____

_____

_____

_____

_____

_____

_____

Freedom Beyond Family Imprints

So far in this Bible Study you have learned primarily about strongholds/curses/hurts that you have direct control over. In this lesson, you will learn about curses that existed before you were born. You may have been drawn to certain sins and never understood why. In this lesson you will learn how to have victory over family sin patterns.

1. What are strongholds? Anything that prevents you from:
    a. truly _____ the Lord
    b. walking in the _____ and _____ that God desires for you.

> *"The weapons of warfare are not carnal, but mighty through God to the pulling down of strongholds: Casting down imaginations and every high thing that exalts itself against the knowledge of God and bringing into captivity every thought to the obedience of Christ."*
>
> **2 Corinthians 10: 4-5**

2. What is the Biblical basis for Family Imprints?

> *"For I, the Lord your God, am a jealous God, visiting the iniquity of the fathers upon the children to the third and fourth generation of those who hate Me, but showing love to a thousand generations of those who love Me and keep My commandments."*
>
> **Deuteronomy 5: 9b-10**
>
> *"Behold I was brought forth in iniquity, and in sin did my mother conceive me."*
>
> **Psalms 51: 5**

3. Three ways Family Imprints/strongholds may enter your life:
   a. At the time of _____ (original sin).
   b. Through your _____.
   c. By _____ the sin patterns of your parents. If you have Freemasonry in your bloodline, see page 237.

Examples: Genesis 12: 10-20 Abram and Sarai
               Genesis 26: 7 Isaac and Rebekah
               Genesis 27 Jacob and Esau

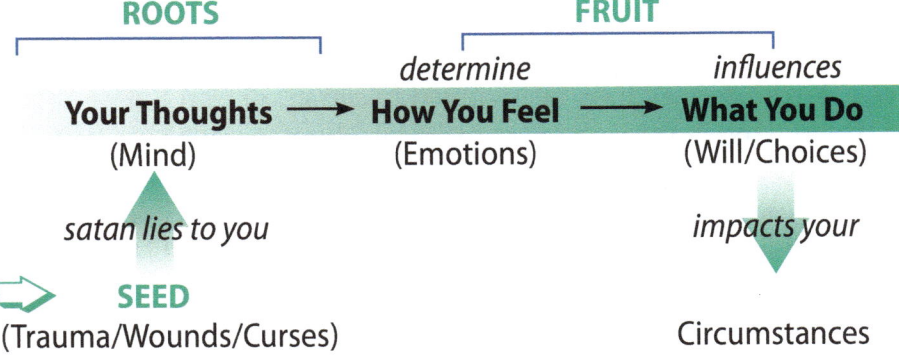

ROOTS   **FRUIT**

determine   *influences*

Your Thoughts → **How You Feel** → **What You Do**
(Mind)   (Emotions)   (Will/Choices)

satan lies to you   *impacts your*

SEED
(Trauma/Wounds/Curses)   Circumstances

4. Family Imprints Patterns can be thought of like a _____ in your life.
   a. The Family Imprints is like the bulb.
   b. The sin pattern is like the stem.

The sin pattern actually produces the right conditions for the fruit to be produced. The fruit is the part of the problem that is produced by sin and can often be seen above the surface or in your actions/behavior.

5. There are two gardens.

Words produce after their kind - good or bad, blessing or cursing. Every word is a seed and there will be a harvest. What kind of harvest do you want?

    a.   Garden of _____ is where the good seeds are sown as you speak those good seeds out of your mouth. Examples include: praise to THEM, encouragement, love and all words that will live in Heaven. These will produce a wonderful harvest for not only you but to whomever you are speaking with.

Father God is your Vine-dresser, the One Who tends your Garden of Life that keeps you connected to Him.

"I am a true sprouting vine, and the farmer who tends the vine is my Father. He cares for the branches connected to Me by lifting and propping up the fruitless branches and pruning every fruitful branch to yield a greater harvest. The words I have spoken over you have already cleansed you. So you must remain in life-union with Me, for I remain in life-union with you. For as a branch severed from the vine will not bear fruit, so your life will be fruitless unless you live your life intimately joined to Mine. "I am the sprouting vine and you're My branches. As you live in union with Me as your source, fruitfulness will stream from within you—But if you live in life-union with Me and if My words live powerfully within you—then you can ask whatever you desire and it will be done. When your lives bear abundant fruit, you demonstrate that you are My mature disciples who glorify My Father!"

John 15:1-5, 7-8

b. Garden of _____ is where all the bad seeds are sown as you let those bad seeds come out of your mouth. These include lies, inner vows, gossip, demeaning words, cussing, but most of all words that will not live in heaven. They are words from the pit of hell. You want your garden of death to always be in a drought ridden state because your mouth is a Heavenly only mouth.

"—but when you live separated from Me you are powerless. If a person is separated from Me, he is discarded; such branches are gathered up and thrown into the fire to be burned."

John 15: 6

"By their fruit you will recognize them. Do people pick grapes from thornbushes, or figs from thistles? Likewise every good tree bears good fruit, but a bad tree bears bad fruit. A good tree cannot bear bad fruit, and a bad tree cannot bear good fruit. Every tree that does not bear good fruit is cut down and thrown into the fire. Thus, by their fruit you will recognize them."

Matthew 7: 16-20

5. Why only "picking the fruit" doesn't work . . .
    a. If you only change your behavior (fruit), you may experience some freedom but only for a short period of time.
    b. The truth is the root issue to the problem (which can be a family imprint) has not been dealt with. The only thing that was dealt with was the fruit.

 **The family sin pattern does not take root until it's activated. Family Imprints are never the root. It's when the sin was activated that it became rooted in you. In order for complete inner healing to take place, you must first deal with the root issue, then deal with the sin pattern.**

What was your memory that first activated the sin?

_____
_____
_____
_____
_____
_____

Remember, the family sin pattern is what creates certain tendencies and desires. Your own choice to sin is then what activates the sin pattern. It's always your choice to choose obedience or to sin. Every word spoken is a prophetic word whether it is positive or negative.

Biblical Examples of Family Imprints

The 27th and the 28th chapters of the book of Deuteronomy are chapters about blessings and curses. Listed below you will find some of the basic areas which cause curses, along with some of the basic effects of curses:

Basic Areas of Family Imprints Curses:

Deuteronomy 27:16-17	Finances
27:16	Rebellion
27:17	Dishonesty
27:18	Cruelty
27:19	Taking unfair advantage
27:20-23	Sexual
27:24-25	Violence
Malachi 3:8-9	Robbing God

Basic Effects of Family Imprints Curses:

Deuteronomy 28:16-17	Finances
28:18	Fruit of the womb
28:19	Home
28:20	Confusion (mental illness)
28:21-22	Sickness and disease
28:23	Unanswered prayer
28:24	Land/drought
28:25, 30-34	Defeat
28:35	Disease
28:36-37	Enslaved to evil
28:38-40	Labor of hands not prosper
28:41	Broken Relationships
28:43-44	Poverty

Curses were carried by Jesus on the cross. He became a curse for us so we could go free.

Family Imprint Example: Spirit of Beguilement

Beguilement, a form of deception, trickery or charm, can have profound and lasting imprint on its victims. When this spirit enters a family dynamic and individuals are misled or manipulated, it can have profound and damaging consequences. Beguilement in families is when someone intentionally tricks or deceives others. This can cause a lot of problems, like:

- Broken trust: Family members may stop believing each other.
- Emotional distress: Being deceived or manipulated can cause deep emotional trauma.
- Relationship damage: People might feel hurt, angry, or scared.
- Family breakdown: Family members become estranged which can lead to divorce.

Therefore I will block her path with thorn bushes; I will wall her in so that she cannot find her way. She will chase after her lovers but not catch them; she will look for them but not find them. Then she will say, 'I will go back to my husband as at first, for then I was better off than now.'

Hosea 2:6-7

 **Personal Application/Exercise**

The specific consequences of beguilement can vary widely depending on the circumstances and the individuals involved. However, the overall imprint is often negative, leading to pain, suffering, and the breakdown of family bonds.

Write down any examples of beguilement you experienced in your family.

_____

_____

_____

Healing Prayer to Break the Spirit of Beguilement:

Father God, I come against the spirit of beguilement in my life. That spirit has a seducing mode of operation that I no longer want to be controlled by. It enticed me and led me away from proper conduct and following You. I sever every assignment of this spirit that is causing me to act in ungodly ways (list the ungodly ways)

_____. *Please forgive me for the ways I've sinned. I receive your forgiveness that the blood of Jesus paid for.*

I break off the spirit of beguilement that causes spiritual blindness and I command the scales to be removed from my eyes and open up my spiritual eyes to see the truth. Holy Spirit show me the lies I believed because of beguilement: _____.

What is the Your Truth about those lies: _____.

I bind the beguilement spirt and the spirit of chaos with the blood of Jesus and send them back to the pits of hell where it came from. I cancel their assignments against me.

I command a hedge of protection from Hosea 2:6-7 against this spirit of beguilement that tried to ruin my life. I receive in exchange from Heaven the spirit of holiness and happiness to take beguilement's place. Thank You for Your Shalom Peace from Heaven to break beguilement's chaos in my life and in my family. Amen!

Prayer to Rid Yourself of the Beguilement Spirit (if this applies):

Father God, do I have the beguilement spirit attached to me? Listen. I command in the name of Jesus and by His blood that any beguilement spirit around me in any way, which is the work of the enemy against me, I am no longer in agreement with you beguilement spirit. I cast you out of my environment with the blood of Jesus. I send you to the foot of the cross where Jesus defeated you. Jesus lives in me and therefore you are no longer in me. I announce and decree on ____(date)____that I am free from the beguilement spirit.

Jesus what do you give me in exchange for this?
_____. Jesus, I accept this supernatural exchange deep within my inner core (my 3 brains: my heart, my life and my future) in Jesus name and by His blood that bought this for me. Amen.

*"See, I set before you today life and prosperity, death
and destruction. For I command you today to love the
LORD your God, to walk in His ways, and to keep His
commands, decrees and laws; then you will live and
increase, and the LORD your God will bless you in
the land you are entering to possess. But if your heart
turns away and you are not obedient, and if you are
drawn away to bow down to other gods and worship
them, I declare to you this day that you will certainly
be destroyed. You will not live long in the land you are
crossing the Jordan to enter and possess. This day I call
heaven and earth as witnesses against you that I have
set before you life and death, blessings and curses. Now
choose life, so that you and your children may live."*

Deuteronomy 30: 15-19

6. Are there Generational Curses?

Often wounded people say "…the reason I have problems in life
has to be coming from generational curses." I do not believe in
generational curses, because the blood of Jesus stopped that for
you when you accepted Him as your personal Lord and Savior. He
became the curse for you according to:

*"Christ redeemed us from the curse of the law by
becoming a curse for us, for it is written: 'cursed is
everyone who is hung on a tree.' "*

Galatians 3:13

The _____of Jesus, that He shed, severed that curse off our
ancestor's sins from us. He became a curse but at the same time He
dissolved the generational curse. It is part of the provision His
journey here on earth purchased for you. With His Work of giving
His Life He destroyed the work of the enemy in your life. A curse
is the work of the enemy.

7. Family _____ influence your attitudes, your moods, your thinking, your speaking, your actions and behaviors. What does that look like? A Family Imprint is much like a fingerprint that influences every area of your life. A fingerprint has many swirls to identify who you are and you leave fingerprints behind as you live your life.

Your ancestors, and this can include those in your life who are authority figures, imprint your life. This begins from your conception (as you learned from the last lesson) and can cause you deep pain and problems up to the present time in your life. Imprints are most powerful during your formative years when your personality is being shaped.

Problems don't come from generational curses but from Family Imprints that need soul healing. Your Family Imprint may have good and bad parts to it. Imprints are left by people in your life who have healed souls (the wise) but is also impacted by those with their own unresolved wounds, lies, beliefs, records of wrongs, inner vows, sin patterns, ways of discipline, ingrained behaviors and influences of all kinds (the unhealed).

Here are some lies that may be in your family's belief systems that can imprint you. These get passed down from generation to generation:

1. God is waiting for me to do something wrong so He can punish me.
2. God made me sick to teach me a lesson.
3. God took my child because He needed another angel.
4. My father/mother died because it wasn't His will to heal him/her.
5. God is disappointed in me.

We call these lies the "Angry God Theory." The Truth is Father God is not angry. A person who acted out any of the above lies towards you as a child would have assisted the enemy in implanting the lie that Father God is abusive.

Personal Application/Exercise

1. What are some lies from my family's belief system?

_____

_____

_____

_____

2. What "Angry God" lies I've inherited from my family's imprint?

_____

_____

_____

_____

Here is the Truth about God:

> *"But I lavish unfailing love for a thousand generations on those who love Me and obey My commands."*
>
> **Exodus 20:6** (NLT)
>
> *"So then, surrender to God. Stand up to the devil and resist him and he will turn and run away from you."*
>
> **James 4:7**

This verse is not complicated, as you surrender your problems to Him. Your surrender becomes your resistance against the enemy. This simple act keeps you in perfect peace which is beyond your understanding.

The verse Ephesians 6:12 puts it this way. You are not fighting against flesh and blood which is what a human is, but you fight against the bad spirits that influence or even possess the person that you are having a problem with. Sometimes that negative interaction can be with yourself which is called self-talk.

8. The Disordered Mind versus the Peaceful Mind

Certain professionals label people with mental disorders but their behavior might actually stem from family imprints and chaos in their life.

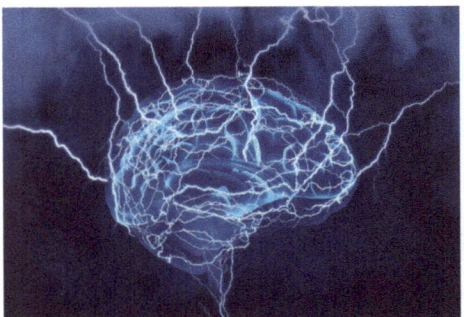

The difference between a disease and a _____ is that you can control a disorder, unlike a disease. Your choices are key. Focusing on healthy thoughts leads to mental health, while unhealthy thinking generates negative behavior. The science of thought shows that your brain can be rewired by your thoughts.

A disordered mind is messy and chaotic, causing unpleasant feelings. Unhealthy thinking leads to neurochemical chaos in the brains, causing degenerative changes and physical/chemical alterations. This creates a sense of being out of control and discontent. Dwelling on toxic thoughts intensifies the feeling.

Neither the brain nor the body is naturally wired for anything toxic. Breaking thinking patterns is crucial to separating yourself from guilt and condemnation. Your key to mental health is to renew your mind and receive guidance from Holy Spirit, just as you've been doing in this course.

You may try to regain control over the chaos and disorder by engaging in various behaviors. This could include actions like swearing, avoiding conversation, restricting food, self-harm, repetitive handwashing, or constant checking of things. These manifestations attempt to restore order and control in the face of mental disorder but do NOT automatically mean you have a mental disorder (contrary to some professionals).

Great news! The power of your thoughts can change your body. You are not a _____ of your body. You can triumph over your biology.

Scientific research shows us that 75-98% of mental, physical and emotional illnesses today comes from toxic thinking. Sin is voluntary as no one forces you to sin. Trauma is involuntary and can be healed.[1]

Unfortunately sin and trauma can look the same. This is why you have to acknowledge your sin and trauma/wounds and then forgive those who've wronged you (or yourself) and give it all to God. When you forgive you get those toxins out of your head, heart, and gut brains. What you keep inside of your brains affects your body.

> *"Out of the same mouth we pour out words of praise one minute and curses the next. My brothers and sisters, this should never be!"*
>
> **James 3:10**

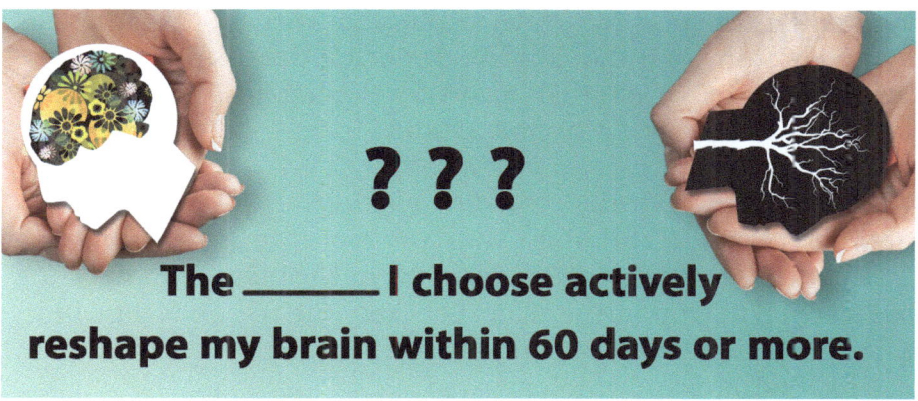

? ? ?

The _____ I choose actively reshape my brain within 60 days or more.

God is the true mind regulator and His Word is better than medications or support groups. His Word is a medicine that washes away every mental sickness.

Your thoughts occupy mental real-estate that produces fruit and that fruit comes from what you say and do. If you plant healthy thoughts then you have mental health but if you plant unhealthy thoughts you will have mental ill health. Unhealthy thoughts create chaos and a disordered mind. Let's look at the roots of this issue.

Dr. Caroline Leaf shares the Dirty Dozen Toxic Roots that plants a sea of trees in your life[(2)]:

Toxic thoughts   Toxic faith   Toxic emotions
Toxic love   Toxic choices
Toxic seriousness   Toxic dreams
Toxic health   Toxic seeds   Toxic schedules
Toxic words   Toxic touch

Dr. Leaf's research shows that a significant portion of health issues may stem from your thought life. However, there is hope. Breaking the cycle of toxic thinking and developing healthy patterns can bring peace to your troubled mind.

When traumatic experiences define relationships and daily functioning, it's crucial to address the toxic roots causing this ongoing trauma. These roots aren't meant to be in the brains and need to be removed to stop further damage. Everyone responds differently, as we are each unique, but addressing the trauma is essential for personal healing and wholeness.

Does any of the toxic roots above resonate with you? If so, please list them.

_____
_____
_____
_____
_____
_____
_____
_____

Personal Application/Exercise

For your well-being, it's important to identify and remove toxic roots. Look at the toxic roots shown in the graphic and write down which roots you may have been impacted by. If you can recall a memory of an incident where you may have taken in that toxic root, write that memory down.

_____

_____

_____

_____

"To appoint unto them that mourn in Zion, to give unto them beauty for ashes, the oil of joy for mourning, the garment of praise for the spirit of heaviness; that they might be called trees of righteousness, the planting of the Lord, that He might be glorified."

Isaiah 61:3

The events in your life cause your disordered mind and Holy Spirit wants to do a process with you to teach you to bring your thoughts into captivity. He wants you to have dominion over your thought life so that you can live an abundant life in Him John

10:10). This verse has the intent of the enemy and the intent of God in it for your life. Life happens and you can choose to come into agreement with the enemy which causes the toxic roots or you can choose to come into agreement with God who gives abundant life. It's your choice.

> *"If you listen to these commands of the LORD your God that I am giving you today, and if you carefully obey them, the LORD will make you the head and not the tail, and you will always be on top and never at the bottom."*
> **Deuteronomy 28:13 NLT**

You control your brain through your mind. Your brain does not control you.

God designed your physical body with three brains and your body has all of these backup systems to warn you when you're not thinking correctly. A backup system is a discomfort zone which often is a physical experience in your body. It may look like your heart beating faster, pounding, the adrenalin rushing, and feel fuzzy in your head. These are God's warning signs that something is not quite right with you. You are no longer in the peace of God.

You may experience this when you are not making good decisions and choices. You may also experience disorder in your mind because you're stepping out of alignment and not listening to HIM. How does your body know this? Because your mind controls your brains. If you pay attention and allow your mind to control your brains, you will make good choices and decisions. Your brains and body obey your mind.

It does not matter how far you've gone with a disordered mind, into this wrong zone of thinking because God makes all things new through replacing what Jesus did for you at the cross and He will make all things new in your mind, your three brains and your body.

 ## Hiding Place Activation

Before we get started, let's add some of your findings from this lesson here so you can deal with them. From page 83, What family sin patterns need to be addressed:

_____

_____

_____

_____

*Sit quietly in a comfortable position. Close your eyes the entire time in a posture of prayer. Remember there will be a lot of quiet time during this activation to allow you to get there. So just relax in HIS Presence.

* Let's take several deep breaths, letting them out slowly. Again breathe in, breathe out.

First, I'm going to pray Psalm 31: 20 over you: *So hide all Your beloved ones in the sheltered, secret hiding place before Your face. Overshadow them by Your glory-presence…Tuck them safely away in the tabernacle where You dwell.*

I want you to say: *Lord, I want You/ to take me back/ to our hiding place now.* Then go back with Him. Just rest in His Presence and love.

Now I'm going to pray Scriptures over you about Family Imprints:

"For I, the Lord your God, am a jealous God, visiting the iniquity of the fathers upon the children to the third and fourth generation of those who hate Me, but showing love to a thousand generations of those who love Me and keep My commandments." Deuteronomy 5: 9b-10

"Behold I was brought forth in iniquity, and in sin did my mother conceive me." Psalms 51: 5

"So then, surrender to God. Stand up to the devil and resist him and he will turn and run away from you." James 4:7

"Today I have given you the choice between life and death, between blessings and curses. Now I call on heaven and earth to witness the choice you make. Oh, that you would choose life, so that you and your descendants might live!" Deuteronomy 30:19

Praying Scripture Prior to Healing:

We are going to pray from Psalm 139: 23-24 TPT. Say out loud after me: *"God, I invite Your searching gaze into my heart. Examine me through and through; find out everything that may be hidden within me. Put me to the test and sift through all my anxious cares. See if there is any path of pain I'm walking on, and lead me back to Your glorious, ever-lasting ways – the path that brings me back to You."*

Now, we're going to invite Holy Trinity to show the Family Imprints He wants to deal with first. Repeat after me: *Holy Trinity, I need Your answers to what Family Imprints have negatively impacted my life.*

1. Ask THEM *what are some lies that are my family's belief systems that have negatively impacted me?* Write them down.

_____

_____

_____

Now ask Him: *Jesus, please show me the pain that this family belief system has cost me in my life.* Write down what you hear/see/sense.

_____

_____

_____

What is Your Truth about that belief? Write it down.

_____

_____

_____

Healing Prayer to Break Family Imprints/ Curses

In the Name of Jesus Christ, I identify the family imprint of____(name one at a time)_____. I forgive the past generations for walking in this particular imprint and for bringing judgment/pain on me (and my family). I seek forgiveness for all the way(s) I have walked in this sin pattern. I break the power of the family imprint/curse of _____(name family imprint)___in the Name and by the Blood of Jesus Christ (touch both hands where the nails would have gone through in the crucifixion) *and I place the cross of Jesus Christ between the curse and myself*. I renounce any level of demonization that exists as a result of this family imprint. I make the choice to walk away from that family imprint and walk in obedience+. I believe and receive the Truth from the Holy Trinity for my life_____(truth)_____ and I will walk that out in my life. Amen.* Clap because the work is finished!

Add if applies: *I also forgive ____(name)____ who abused me in this area.*

* Placing the cross in prayer between you and an area of sin is a type of symbolic or visual prayer. If the cross is between you and the sin, then you have to go back through the cross to pick the sin up again.

+ This may mean not to drink alcohol, buy pornographic materials, or whatever else the sin may be.

2. Holy Trinity what are some mental dis-eases that I've been diagnosed with?

_____

_____

Ask THEM, where does this diagnosis/lie come from?

_____

_____

What is Your Truth for my life going forward?

_____

_____

Now ask Him: *Jesus, please show me the pain that this family imprint diagnosis has cost me in my life.* Write down what you hear/see/sense.

_____

_____

_____

Finally, I want you to declare Philippians 4:8 over your life. I've revised the verse to be in first person.

I commit to keeping my thoughts continually fixed on (point to heaven) *all/that is authentic and real, honorable and admirable, beautiful and respectful, pure and holy, merciful and kind. And I fasten my thoughts* (touch your head) *on every glorious work of God, praising Him always. Amen*

DON'T KEEP THE SECRET!

Healing Prayer to Break Toxic Roots

Go back to page 90 where you identified toxic roots. Look at the toxic roots and write down which roots you have been impacted by. If you can recall a memory of an incident where you may have taken in that toxic root, write that down as well.

Now we'll go through the process of casting your cares upon Him by giving Him your toxic family roots, recognizing that every wrong action was already taken care of, by Him, on the cross.

In the Divine Exchange you will allow Him to take what He paid for. You'll release events that may feel overwhelming. You give THEM your burdens, and in return, He exchanges your ashes for beauty.

Get in your prayer position. Now we're ready to cut your Toxic Roots.

In the name of Jesus Christ I confess that I have born bad fruit from the toxic root of _____(toxic root)_____. *I give You the pain it has cost me* ____(tell Him your pain)____. *Jesus, what is Your Truth in exchange for my toxic root?* _____(His Truth - write it down)____. *I make the choice to forgive* _____(names of people)_____ *who gave me those roots. I ask you, Jesus, to forgive me for believing that toxic root was mine.*

I break (clap) *the power* (fist pump) *of this toxic root* _____(toxic root)____ *in the name of Jesus Christ and His blood* (touch crucifixion nail holes). *I sever it with the Sword of the Spirit* (use the sword of the Spirit and sever it). *It can no longer hurt or damage my life. I renounce any demonization that exists as a result of my toxic root. Now I turn my back* (turn around) *on this root and choose instead to believe* _____ (truth)_____ *and I can walk it out in the powerful* (pump your first) *name of Jesus Christ. Amen so let it be.* Clap!

Casting your cares upon Him means giving Him your toxic family imprint roots, recognizing that every wrong action was already taken care of, by Him, on the cross. By allowing Him to take what He paid for, you release events that may feel overwhelming. You're giving God your burdens, and in return, He exchanges your ashes for beauty.

OPTIONAL: Family Tree Prayer. If you are still convinced that generational curses are upon you, please visualize JESUS on the cross. Then say this prayer out loud:

Healing Family Tree Prayer:

Jesus, Here I am in YOU and YOU are in me. I have a concern about my ancestor's past that I believe has passed down to me. Others do not need this but I do, so for my peace I am bringing my problem for YOU to resolve. I want YOU to scrub (scrub your tree) *my family tree on all sides with YOUR blood* (touch crucifixion nail holes), *all the way back to Adam and Eve. Please let me see YOU do this work for my peace of mind* (peace sign), *removing any spoken word curses* (pull out the curses from your mind), *intentional or unintentional. Let YOUR blood* (touch nail holes) *remove any passed down works of the enemy that would be influencing me in any way. Let Your blood* (touch nail holes) *remove any family diseases, or addictions as You scrub* (scrub it) *my tree, removing all drama, trauma, poisons and wounds that would in any way affect me.*

Thank YOU Jesus for YOUR work in the Garden of Gethsemane, during all of YOUR sufferings, at the hands of the brutal soldiers, on the cross, into the grave, YOUR trip into hell, in the tomb and then YOUR resurrection and Your Victorious exit. Thank YOU (thumbs up) *for doing this for me. Today on_____ (today's date)_____ I am establishing a prophetic path of decreeing and proclaiming that I can walk with the HOLY TRINITY, that I am free from my past ancestors and anything they have done, said or any contracts they may have signed. This umbilical cord that was nurturing me, is now cut apart* (sever it with the sword of the Spirit) *removing all assignments of the dark kingdom against me. In the name of Jesus and by HIS blood* (touch nail holes) *that bought this for me. Amen.*

> **Thou shalt also decree a thing, and it shall be established unto thee: and the light shall shine upon thy ways.**
>
> **Job 22:28**

Breakthrough Decrees (repeat daily)
(activate your words with body action)

1. God redeemed me from all Family Imprints (Galatians 3:13). I walk in faith and bear good fruit (Matthew 7:16-20).

2. I walk in godly patterns in my life choosing life and blessings (Deuteronomy 30:19).

3. I have a covenant with God, and by the blood of Jesus I release my divine protection and divine provision (Hebrews 8:6).

4. And I speak to this day and I call you blessed. And I declare that I serve a mighty God who today will do exceedingly and abundantly beyond all that I can ask or think (Ephesians 3:20). I say you are a good God and I eagerly anticipate your goodness today.

5. Each of my family members is wonderfully blessed and radically loves Jesus (Acts 16:30-31).

6. My truth to replace the lie:_____

On this day _____, I establish these decrees that are founded in God's Word.

Signed: _____

Homework This Week

1. Say out loud this week's Breakthrough Decrees daily with physical activation.

2. If you want to debrief with someone, find a trusted friend who can listen to and support you through the Family Imprint lessons learned. Often, it is best to just soak in worship music. Graham Cooke has some excellent YouTube videos. We recommend: *The #1 reason God is not disappointed with you...*

3. If you have a healthy relationship with a family member, show them the Toxic Root Family Tree and ask them what roots may be problematic. Use the Healing Prayer to rid yourself of those roots.

4. Write in your Victory Journal and Daily Gratitude Journal.

5. Join the weekly live Mentoring Moment.

Resources

(1) We tried to ask a basic question that hasn't been asked: Is there any common biological basis for mental illness?" Amit Etkin, MD, PhD Assistant Professor of Psychiatry and Behavioral Sciences Stanford University Investigator, Sierra Pacific Mental Illness Research Education and Clinical Center (MIRECC).

(2) Dr. Caroline Leaf's SWITCH app and book, 21 Day Detox. She has many resources on her website and books on amazon. All of them are excellent resources for this topic.

(3) You may want to soak in worship music. Graham Cooke has some excellent YouTube videos. We recommend: *The #1 reason God is not disappointed with you...*

Victory Journal of Your Progress

You may want to make a list of the Family Imprints you have broken as a reminder to your inner healing progress:

Family Imprints:

_____   _____

_____   _____

_____   _____

_____   _____

_____   _____

_____   _____

_____   _____

_____   _____

_____   _____

_____   _____

Use additional pages if you need more room.

Family Blessings I Am Thankful For:

_____   _____
_____   _____
_____   _____
_____   _____
_____   _____
_____   _____
_____   _____
_____   _____
_____   _____
_____   _____

Use additional pages if you need more room.

Daily Gratitude Journal

Write down 3 things you are thankful or grateful for each day.

Date:_____ 1. _____
2. _____
3. _____
Date:_____ 1. _____
2. _____
3. _____
Date:_____ 1. _____
2. _____
3. _____
Date:_____ 1. _____
2. _____
3. _____
Date:_____ 1. _____
2. _____
3. _____

Date:_____1. _____

2. _____

3. _____

Date:_____1. _____

2. _____

3. _____

Date:_____1. _____

2. _____

3. _____

Date:_____1. _____

2. _____

3. _____

Fill-in-the-Blank Answer Guide

1. a. loving, b. victory, blessings
3. a. conception b. genes c. walking in
4. tulip bulb
5. a. Life, b. Death
6. blood
7. Imprints
8. disorder
   victim
   thoughts

The circular diagram in the image reads:

When Others Curse You · Bitter Root Judgments · Family Imprints · Inner Vows · Breaking Soul Ties · In Utero Trauma

Where was God?
Body, Soul & Spirit

5

Breaking Your Inner Vows

As you've already learned, how you think and speak is so very important along with your self-talk. Inner vows are the most crucial determinant of how you think, speak and act in your life. Your inner vow becomes the IV put into your body and soul by the enemy. This IV poisons you and destroys Jeremiah 29:11 in your life. It limits what the Holy Trinity can do for you.

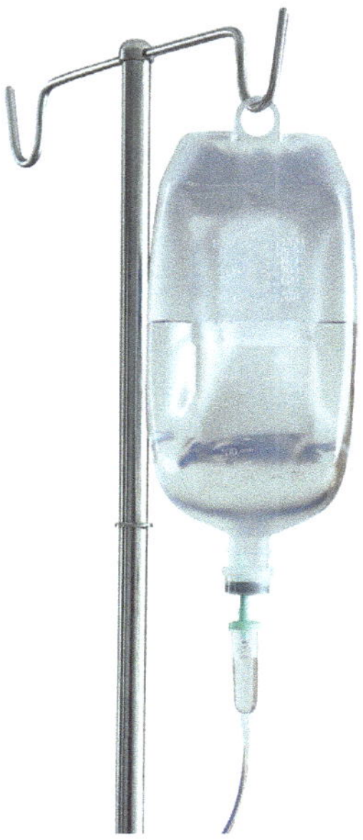

"For as he thinks in his heart so he is."
Proverbs 23:7 (AKJV)

Your thinking rules your life and must be positive and aligned with Heaven because you are in the world but not of the world. You are an ambassador to this world to be salt and light for the Kingdom of God. If your words and thoughts cannot live in heaven, you must get rid of them here on earth.

Personal Self-Assessment

What are some common thoughts you have?

_____

_____

_____

_____

_____

Do I need to change how I think? Yes / No

An inner vow is a self-vow that comes out of a traumatizing situation. When you are traumatized you make a meaning about the situation that turns into an inner vow to protect yourself in the future. THEY are your Protector and you don't need to do THEIR job. This is a trust issue with THEM which is a heart brain issue.

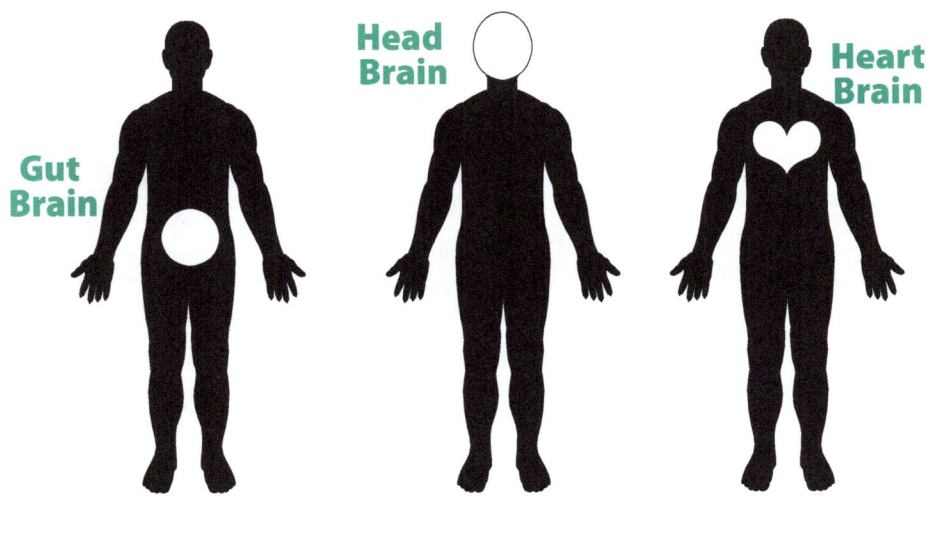

Not only are you woven by THEM in three parts like THEY are, yet you are still one, just like THEM.

You also have many threes in you. These are:

a. Three parts of you made up of your Body, Soul and Spirit
b. Three Brains: Gut Brain which is your Body, Head Brain which is your Soul (mind, will and emotions), Heart Brain which is your Spirit
c. Three thrones: Throne of your Body, Throne of your Soul and the Throne of your Spirit

1. Three Thrones

You have three thrones and you get to _____ who sits there. If you want true freedom you will ask Holy Trinity to sit on all three thrones. This is the way you stay away from your old vomit (i.e. lies, ways of thinking, ugly behavior...). This prevents double-mindedness.

It is very easy to give the Holy Trinity your Heart Throne (Spirit) yet close THEM out of your Throne of your Soul and Body. That is why you do things you do not want to do and struggle with being double minded when it comes to being soul ruled or Spirit ruled. When THEY are given these Thrones to rule, that is where you find the Promised Land of True Rest in THEM.

> *"Now the promise of entering into God's rest is still for us today. So we must be extremely careful to ensure that we all embrace the fullness of that promise and not fail to experience it."*
>
> **Hebrews 4:1**

Your thinking is the greatest key to keeping the Holy Trinity sitting on the Throne of each area of you. It is imperative that you take every thought captive, because then, the right words of life will come from your mouth into the Garden of Life for a good harvest.

So take the Personal Self- Assessment to see where you stand in the NOW. You will ask THEM about Who sits on the Throne of your Body, Throne of your Mind and the Throne of your Spirit. You will be taking this Assessment so you have a starting point to see where you stand, in the Hiding Place Activation, after you gain the knowledge of these tools from this chapter.

 **Personal Self-Assessment**

Ask these questions of Holy Trinity (we will address this in the Hiding Place Activation):

1. *Father God, Jesus and Holy Spirit, Who sits on the Throne of my heart?* Wait for THEIR answer. Please write down your answer.

_____

_____

_____

2. *Father God, Jesus and Holy Spirit: Who sits on the Throne of my Mind?* Wait for THEIR answer. Please write down your answer.

_____

_____

_____

3. *Father God, Jesus and Holy Spirit: Who sits on the Throne of my Body?* Wait for THEIR answer. Please write down your answer.

_____

_____

_____

If you want to live a victorious, happy life, you must give THEM permission to occupy all three of your thrones.

2. Have you given your power over to _____? How do you worship fear? That worship sounds like fear coming out of your mouth. Examples: I have anxiety or a panic attack, I'm stressed, I can't take any more, not one more punch. I'm done with this crap happening to me.

Here are some Symptoms of the FEAR Door that you can open up to the enemy. Check any that apply to you:
- ❑ Anxiety
- ❑ Depression
- ❑ Panic attacks
- ❑ Traumatic events
- ❑ Poverty
- ❑ Feeling of being an Orphan/on the outside looking in/never fitting
- ❑ True Identity problem
- ❑ Controlling to feel safe
- ❑ Fear of people
- ❑ Fear of evil
- ❑ Fear of the future
- ❑ Fear of fear
- ❑ Fear of relapse
- ❑ Fear of God's judgement
- ❑ Drugs and medications
- ❑ Fear of disease
- ❑ Fear of sexuality
- ❑ Other _____.

You may have a battle going on in your mind and then fear comes and sits with you on the throne of your mind.

Here are four tools for you to use against fear:

1. You have power over fear because it's given to you by THEM. Fear is <u>F</u>alse <u>E</u>vidence <u>A</u>ppearing <u>R</u>eal. Fear does not exist unless you give it power to exist in your life. Don't give fear your power.

2. Know the perfect love of Jesus

3. The mind of Christ has how much fear in it? None. YOU have the mind of Christ.

4. YahWeh breathing. It has been said that the Jewish sages associated the covenant name of God, **Yahweh**, with breath. The idea is that the name itself, when pronounced, is the sound of breathing: the two syllables of the name correspond to the intake and outtake of a single breath. In this way, our breaths evoke the name of God. A naturally voiced inhalation sounds like "Yah," and a voiced exhalation sounds like "Weh." Thus, with every breath we take, we are speaking God's name. He breathed into us the breath of life (Genesis 2:7), and we still retain that breath.

Yah Weh breathing can help with anxiety, depression, managing stress, improving focus and better sleep.

During our Hiding Activation you'll have the opportunity to ask Jesus to take your power over fear away from fear and wash it in His blood for purity's sake and give it back to you. When you allow THEM to sit on all three thrones and partner with you, you'll be ready to navigate life well with THEIR true joy in your life.

Questions to Ask Yourself When Fear Comes in:
- Will the thoughts I'm having about fear, be in the mind of Jesus Christ?
- Holy Spirit have I given my power over to fear?
- Have I made fear bigger than You? When you make something bigger than Jesus it becomes an idol. Show me what You want to do with this idol, Jesus?
- Jesus let me see how You see fear?

> **"Life and death is in the power of the tongue and you will eat the fruit thereof."**
>
> **Proverbs 18:21**

3. The enemy of your soul wants nothing more than to prevent you from fulfilling your destiny by entangling you with _____ _____.

4. Self-inflicted _____ come from your own belief system.

   a. Self-inflicted curses are made often at an early age from your own _____.

---

b. Self-inflicted curses also come about by the choice not to _____ *and* not to _____ the truth, which is revealed to you in God's Word.

> *"The weapons of warfare are not carnal, but mighty through God to the pulling down of strongholds: Casting down imaginations and every high thing that exalts itself against the knowledge of God and bringing into captivity every thought to the obedience of Christ."*
>
> **2 Corinthians 10: 4-5** (KJV)

5. Inner vows are your belief system about _____.

a. These self-inflicted curses are expressed through your thoughts and words.

b. Inner vows are made to _____ you from being wounded or hurt again. As a result, those vows significantly impact your relationships because that vow influences how you respond in different situations and to other people.

> *"Keep your thoughts continually fixed on all that is authentic and real, honorable and admirable, beautiful and respectful, pure and holy, merciful and kind. And fasten your thoughts on every glorious work of God, praising Him always."*
>
> **Philippians 4: 8** (TPT)

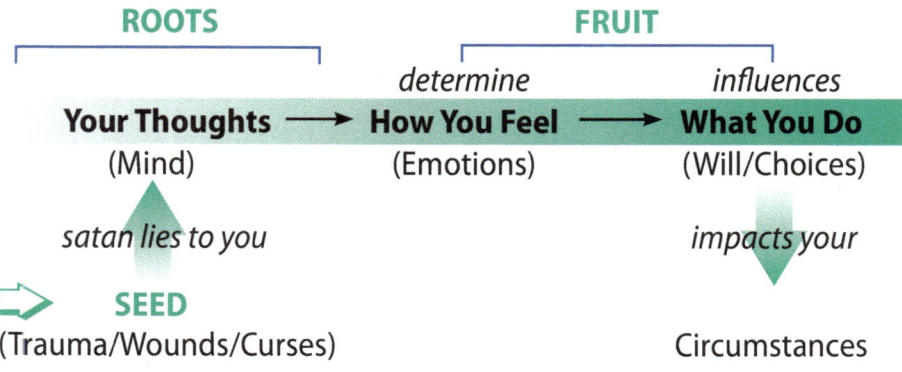

> *Watch your words and be careful what you say, and
> you'll be surprised by how few troubles you'll have.*
>
> **Proverbs 21:23** (TPT)

> *"The tongue has the power of life and death, and those
> who love it will eat its fruit."*
>
> **Proverbs 18:21** (N V)

Dr. Caroline Leaf, author of *Who Switched Off My Brain?* states:
*"Negative words can be more harmful to <u>you</u> than the person you say
them to, because your mind formed the toxic thought, meditated on the
words and spoke them – reinforcing them in your mind.*

*Because you created a negative stronghold, your body reacts
with stress. If the stress chemicals flow in your brain for
longer than **30 seconds**, your thinking, intelligence, body,
and everything else are all going to be negatively affected."*

6. Inner vows prevent you from blessing _____.
    Inner vows begin with the word "I" such as
    - **I** *will never love again.*
    - **I** *will never trust again.*
    - **I** *won't try again.*
    - **I** *hate myself.*
    - **I** *am stupid.*

    a. Inner vows are often what hold the person in the cycle of
        old _____.

    b. Inner vows resist normal _____.

> *"Again, you have heard that it was said to the people
> a long time ago, Do not break your oath, but keep the
> oaths you have made to the Lord." But I tell you, do not
> swear at all: either by heaven, for it is His footstool; or by
> Jerusalem, for it is the city of the Great King."*
>
> **Matthew 5:33** (NIV)

7. The five characteristics of an inner vow

1) A distinctive mark of an inner vow is that it resists the normal _____ process in an individual. 1 Corinthians 13: 11 tells us *"When I was a child, I talked like a child, I reasoned like a child. When I became a man, I put childish ways behind me."*

   Example: Children raised in a home where adults were abusive may create an image within themselves that to become an adult means to become abusive.

You are saying I can't do this or won't do this and that may take away Jeremiah 29:11 from coming to pass in your life. Wrong patterns will repeat over and over again due to inner self vows.

 **Activation Exercise**

Physically stand up and give yourself permission to be a man or woman. Say out loud:

By an act of my will, I give myself permission to become a man/woman. While I can still have fun and enjoy life, I choose to put childish ways behind me. I choose to be responsible. I choose to become the man/woman that God created me to be. Thank you for Holy Spirit's empowerment to change. Amen.

2) Vows that are made as an adult will _____ the person. Vows that are made as a child are _____ the person.

> *"When a woman makes a vow to God and binds herself by a pledge as a young girl still living in her father's house, and her father hears of her vow or pledge but says nothing to her, then she has to make good on all her vows and pledges. But if her father holds her back when he hears of what she has done, none of her vows and pledges are valid. God will release her since her father held her back."*
>
> **Numbers 30: 3-5** (The Message)

This is one of the reasons it is so important for parents to speak _____ into the lives of their children (or any child) whenever they hear an inner vow being expressed.

3) The affects of the child's vow become deeply _____ into the core belief system of the child. The inner vow becomes part of the foundation that the person builds their life choices upon.

Every word is a seed and it brings forth either life or death. Good seed goes into the Garden of God, which is the Garden of Life. Every bad seed goes into the garden of the enemy, which is the garden of death, because he counterfeits everything God does.

When a person is saved through Jesus Christ, these vows remain as _____ _____ that interfere with the process of growing up in the character of Christ. The power of these vows _must_ be broken. This battle is self-inflicted.

4) When an inner vow is made as an adult, it creates conflict but does not become part of the foundation of the person's life. An inner vow made as an adult affects the person's _____ and _____.

Example: Israel's complaining

5) Inner vows may not manifest immediately but often will lie dormant until a person or situation _____ them. Many different things can trigger inner vows that have been dormant. Healing is a continual process. Never assume everything has been taken care of.

If you overreact to a person or situation, it may be that your inner vow, that had laid dormant for years, was suddenly triggered. In life, someone unknowingly can trigger your inner vow. Your hot button reaction really isn't about that person's comment or behavior. The situation has simply unburied one of your inner vows which needs to be healed. You may react to that trigger with the emotions of a child at the age when you were first wounded.

Our inner healing process can be compared to revealing the different layers in an onion – one layer at a time.

Examples of Common Inner Vows that lead to Unhealthy Patterns/Fruit:
Some inner vows are very simple while others are very complex. Others may be hard to understand.

The list could go on and on but these are just a sample of the lies you have vowed to believe and keep believing. Vows put limits in your life that the enemy wants there. A vow you make out of a bad situation will not exist in Heaven so you need to not make inner vows with yourself.

This is how you measure what a vow will do. A vow steals and kills Philippians 4:13, Jeremiah 29:11 and so many of His promises to you in your life. The biggest problem with inner vows is that satan wants you to make them out of a hurtful situation. The reason for this is that your inner vows put up borders that God is fenced in by.

- ❏ I am bad.
- ❏ I am ugly.
- ❏ I am stupid.
- ❏ I am dirty.
- ❏ I hate my body.
- ❏ I hate being a woman (or man).
- ❏ I never want children.
- ❏ I will never love again.
- ❏ I will never trust again.
- ❏ I will never allow myself to be vulnerable.
- ❏ I never want to get married (or remarried).
- ❏ I will never cry.
- ❏ I never want to grow up.
- ❏ My abilities aren't good enough.
- ❏ I will keep the secret.
- ❏ I will never tell anyone the truth about my family.
- ❏ I never want to be like my parent(s).
- ❏ I hate _____.
- ❏ I don't need your help.
- ❏ I cannot succeed.
- ❏ It always happens to me.
- ❏ I have to make you happy.
- ❏ I'll never meet God's standards.
- ❏ Why even try?
- ❏ This is what I deserve.
- ❏ I'll get even.
- ❏ I'll always be afraid.
- ❏ It's hopeless.
- ❏ I'll never change.
- ❏ I can't _____.
- ❏ My faith isn't strong enough.
- ❏ I'll always be lonely.
- ❏ I have nothing to offer.
- ❏ If people only knew…
- ❏ I'll never amount to anything.
- ❏ I'm not worthy.
- ❏ I'll never _____.
- ❏ I always _____.
- ❏ Every time I try, I fail.
- ❏ I don't fit in.
- ❏ I won't share my heart.
- ❏ I never get what I want.
- ❏ I can do it all by myself.
- ❏ Emotions are to be kept to yourself.
- ❏ I always get sick.
- ❏ I have disappointed God.
- ❏ Life will always treat me bad.

8. The process of breaking your inner vows

   a. Identify the event or person in your life that caused you to make the inner vow. Go back to the first time you recall thinking/speaking your inner vow. Ask Holy Spirit to help you recognize what it cost you and the pain you feel.

   b. Choose to forgive the person/people involved. Give your records/account of wrongdoing to Jesus.

   c. Ask God to help you to forgive yourself for believing your inner vow.

   d. Sever the inner vow with the Sword of the Spirit.

   e. Turn your back on your inner vow by choosing the Truth and walking in that Truth.

The Word says to build up yourself in the Lord. This means that you encourage yourself with what God says about you through His promises to you.

Ask Jesus: *Jesus, what specific inner vows have I made that impact my life that You want me to deal with? How am I triggered by others because of these inner vows?*

_____

_____

_____

_____

What records of wrongs have I been holding against others with my inner vows?

_____

_____

_____

_____

_____

_____

_____

_____

 **Hiding Place Activation**

Sit quietly in a comfortable position. Close your eyes the entire time in a posture of prayer. Remember there will be a lot of quiet time during this activation so just relax in His Presence.

Take several deep breaths, letting them out slowly. Again breathe in, breathe out.

Here are some verses related to inner vows to read out loud:

"Do not be deceived. God is not mocked, for whatever a man sows, this he will also reap."
Galatians 6:7

"As a man thinks in his heart so he is."
Proverbs 27:7

"The tongue has the power of life and death, and those who love it will eat its fruit."
Proverbs 18: 21

For although we live in the natural realm, we don't wage a military campaign employing human weapons, using manipulation to achieve our aims. Instead, our spiritual weapons are energized with divine power to effectively dismantle the defenses *behind which people hide. [5] We can demolish every deceptive fantasy that opposes God and break through every arrogant attitude that is raised up in defiance of the true knowledge of God. We capture, like prisoners of war, every thought and insist that it bow in obedience to the Anointed One.*
2 Corinthians 10: 4-5

Watch your words and be careful what you say, and you'll be surprised how few troubles you'll have.
Proverbs 21: 23

First, you're going to pray Psalm 31: 20 over yourself:
[20] *So hide me Your beloved one in the sheltered, secret hiding place before Your face. Overshadow me by Your glory-presence…Tuck me safely away in the tabernacle where You dwell.*

Lord, I want You to take me back to our hiding place now. Go back with Him to your hiding place. Then rest in His Presence and love for as long as you like.

Praying Scripture Prior to Inner Vow Healing:

Pray from Psalm 139:23-24 TPT. Say out loud: *"God, I invite Your searching gaze into my heart. Examine me through and through; find out everything that may be hidden within me. Put me to the test and sift through all my anxious cares. See if there is any path of pain I'm walking on, and lead me back to Your glorious, everlasting ways— the path that brings me back to You."*

Now, you're going to invite Holy Spirit to bring you back to your inner vow: *Jesus, show me where I first made this inner vow_____. Jesus, please show me where You were when I made this inner vow.*

Say: *Holy Spirit, please show me the pain that this inner vow has cost me in my life.*

_____

_____

_____

Holy Spirit, show me what records/account I've been holding on to as a result of this inner vow?

_____

_____

_____

Holy Spirit, show me if I am suffering from any physical, emotional, or mental disease due to my inner vows?

_____

_____

_____

In the name of Jesus Christ I confess that I have believed the inner vow that _____(vow)_____. Jesus, I give you my inner vow of _____(vow)_____ and the pain it has caused me _____ (pain)_____. Jesus, what is Your Truth in exchange for my inner vow? _____(His Truth)_____.

In Jesus Christ's name, I command complete healing and restoration of _
(disease)_____*caused by my inner vow. By Your stripes I am healed
(touch nail holes). Thank you Jesus. I make the choice to forgive* _____
(name)_____*whose sin against me enabled me to make this inner
vow. I ask you, Jesus, to forgive me for believing my inner vow. I give to
You my records/account of wrongdoing (hand records to him). What do
You want to do with these records Jesus?* _____

I break the power of this inner vow _____(vow)_____ *in the
name of Jesus Christ and I sever it (sever it) with the Sword of the Spirit.
What will You give me in exchange for my pain and records?* _____

*I renounce any demonization that exists as a result of my inner vow.
Now I turn my back on this vow and choose instead to believe*
_____(Truth)_____*and I can walk it out in the powerful
name of Jesus Christ.*

Now you have the opportunity to invite Holy Trinity to be on
your thrones over your body, soul and spirit. You may want to re-
view your answers on pages 108-109 as to who is on your thrones
because this is called THEIR proper place in you.

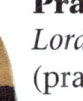

Prayer:

*Lord, I thank You for new revelation in my life. I repent
(praying hands) of being on my thrones when it is NOT
(shake head no) my rightful place. I relinquish to You
(hands up) Holy Trinity my thrones over my (touch
each one) body, soul and spirit and ask that YOU be on these three
thrones.* Bow down to THEM in an act of honor and submission.

Finally, let's address the fear in your life:

*Holy Trinity, I don't want fear in my life. I receive Your unconditional
perfect love (hands in heart position) into my (touch each one) heart
brain, head brain and gut brain and command fear to leave (point
where you want fear to go) my life now in Jesus name. I have the
mind (touch head) of Christ so fear can no (shake head no) longer
be a part of me. I receive (hands out) your shalom to break the chaos
in my (touch each one) body, soul and spirit in Jesus name. I walk in
Your victory.* Stand up and jump up and down with your arms in
the victory pose! *Amen, so let it be!*

I commit (clasp hands) *this day to walk out my healing with Jesus'
help by His blood* (touch crucifixion nail holes) *and in His* (point
up) *powerful name*: Clap!

_____ <signature> _____ <date> _____.

9. Final Tool: You are Seated in Heavenly Places. Throne Room

It's normal to have times you don't feel good emotionally and
physically, BUT, do you stay there focused on your problem?
When we feel down it usually means you're looking at things
from the natural view, not the supernatural view. It is during
those times you need to focus on being seated in Heavenly
places where Holy Trinity is the problem solver for any problem you have. God wants you to live seated in heaven.

> *He raised us up with Christ the exalted One, and we
> ascended with Him into the glorious perfection and
> authority of the heavenly realm, for we are now co-seated
> as One with Christ!*
>
> **Ephesians 2:6**

Here are some questions to ask yourself to see where you are seat-
ed:
- Will this action live in Heaven?
- Will this thought live in Heaven?

What you focus on becomes your reality. What comes to your mind and physical body becomes your reality. When you think and speak it out, the enemy can take your own words and use them against you. Your words create your tomorrow. What fruit are your words producing now?

_____

_____

_____

 ## Breakthrough Decrees (repeat daily)
(activate your words with body action)

1. I am the head, not the tail. I have insight. I have wisdom in my life. I have ideas and divine strategies. I have authority (Deuteronomy 28:13, 8:18; James 1:5-8; Luke 10:19).

2. I expect the best day of my life spiritually, emotionally, relationally and financially in Jesus' name (Romans 15:13).

3. I speak to the raging waters in my life; peace, be still. I say to my mind; peace, be still. I say to my emotions; peace, be still. I say to my body; peace, be still. I say to my home; peace, be still. I say to my family; peace, be still (Mark 4:39).

4. My prayers for my life are powerful and effective (2 Corinthians 5:21; James 6:16b).

5. My angels are carrying out the Word of God on my behalf (Psalm 103:20).

6. My truth to replace the lie:_____

    On this day _____, I establish these decrees that are founded in God's Word.

    Signed: _____

* Declarations used with permission of Steve and Wendy Backlund with IgnitingHope.com

Homework This Week

1. Say out loud this week's Breakthrough Decrees daily.

2. Find someone to share what Inner Vow most negatively impacted your life, the Truth that you received from Jesus, and what steps you are taking to walk in victory. Share one way they can support you in your healing journey with inner vows.

3. New Habit: Try out some new worship music. Example, watch the 12-minute movie "The God Who Sees" (The Rock, The Road, and The Rabbi Foundation) and share your personal take-away.

4. Write in your Victory and Gratitude Journals.

5. Join us on our Mentoring call.

 **Victory Journal of Your Progress**

Write down what victories/wins you experienced this week in your life.

_____

_____

_____

_____

_____

_____

_____

_____

_____

_____

_____

_____

_____

_____

_____

_____

_____

_____

_____

_____

_____

_____

_____

_____

_____

_____

_____

_____

_____

_____

Daily Gratitude Journal

Write down 3 things you are thankful or grateful for each day.

Date:_____1. _____

2. _____

3. _____

Date:_____1. _____

2. _____

3. _____

Date:_____1. _____

2. _____

3. _____

Date:_____1. _____

2. _____

3. _____

Date:_____1. _____

2. _____

3. _____

Date:_____1. _____

2. _____

3. _____

Date:_____1. _____

2. _____

3. _____

Date:_____1. _____

2. _____

3. _____

Fill-in-the-Blank Answer Guide

1. choose
2. fear
3. strongholds
4. curses
   a. woundedness
   b. believe, obey
5.   yourself   protect
6.   you
   a. patterns
   b. change
7. 1) maturing
   2) affect   set   into   truth
   3) rooted   ungodly beliefs
   4) choices, habits
   5) triggers

 **Victory Journal of Your Progress**

You may want to make a list of the Inner Vows you have broken as well as the Truth as a reminder to you of your inner healing progress:

My Inner Vows: God's Truth:

_____   _____
_____   _____
_____   _____
_____   _____
_____   _____
_____   _____
_____   _____
_____   _____
_____   _____
_____   _____
_____   _____
_____   _____
_____   _____
_____   _____
_____   _____
_____   _____
_____   _____
_____   _____
_____   _____
_____   _____
_____   _____
_____   _____
_____   _____
_____   _____
_____   _____
_____   _____
_____   _____

Use additional pages if you need more room.

Gaining Freedom from Bitter Root Judgments

In the last lesson we covered Inner Vows, which prevents you from blessing you. Now you will learn how you prevent others from blessing you. Do you want to be blessed? You may not realize that it may be your own judgments that prevent others from blessing you. In this lesson you will learn how to release your Bitter Root Judgments which may change your personal relationships for the better.

Again, others can unknowingly trigger you because of a bitter root judgment you made as a child or young adult. Until we unearth these bitter roots, it may be like walking on eggshells around you because one never knows when you'll be triggered or why. It's time to dig these bitter roots out and heal the pain so you can love and receive others' love.

> *"Each heart knows its own bitterness and no one else can share the joy."*
>
> **Proverbs 14: 10**
>
> *"See to it that no one misses the grace of God and that no bitter root grows up to cause trouble and defile many."*
>
> **Hebrews 12: 15** (NIV)

1. **Bitter Root Judgments** prevent _____ from blessing _____.

   a. Bitter Root Judgments are made as a result of painful events (or woundedness) in your life. The judgment actually gains strength, even to the point it may become a major _____ in your life.

   ROOTS   **FRUIT**

   determine   *influences*

   Your Thoughts → **How You Feel** → **What You Do**

   (Mind)   (Emotions)   (Will/Choices)

   satan lies to you   *impacts your*

   ⇨ **SEED**
   (Trauma/Wounds/Curses)   Circumstances

   b. Those judgments are like a wall of _____ that you build around your own heart that robs you of the joys of others blessing you. Bitter Root Judgments cause us to "trample on" even the best intentions of others.

Biblical Example: I Samuel 18 — King Saul with David

What wall of bitterness is your heart hiding behind?

_____

_____

_____

2. Walls and Obstructions

The purpose of a wall that you build, with the help of satan's king-dom, is to distance Father God, Jesus and Holy Spirit from you. The walls are made up of inner vows, lies the enemy has sown into you, and lists of wrongs you keep against yourself and others which we call bitter root judgements. These walls can be kept together by anger, fear, resentment and any other emotion that won't live in Heaven.

The enemy feeds you garbage lies so you see the Holy Trinity in these ways (See chapter 2 for more information on Earthly Father Figures/EFFs) :

1. **Father God**: The enemy uses the lens of any EFF who is an authority in your life. He uses these people in your life to distort how you see and feel about Father God. Father God provides materially and emotionally. He protects and gives you your identity.
2. **Holy Spirit**: The enemy uses the lens of your Earthly Mother Figures (EMF) to distort how you see and feel about Holy Spirit. These figures could be anyone that had a motherly role in your life. The Holy Spirit comforts, nurtures, teaches and guides you.

3. **Jesus**: The enemy uses the lens of siblings or others to distort how you see and feel about Jesus. Jesus is your companion and best communicator. He intercedes for you 24/7.

When it comes to Bitter Root Judgments, the enemy will sow lies into your head through your earthly father figures such as:
- My dad doesn't love me so how can my heavenly Father love me.
- My dad says I'm worthless so I believe my heavenly Father believes I'm worthless.

With earthly mother figures the enemy will do the same to keep you from getting close to Holy Spirit, for example:
- My mother told me she hated me and wished I had never been born, so I must have been a mistake.
- My mom abandoned me so I must be unlovable.

With earthly siblings or lack thereof the enemy uses people to distort how you see and feel about Jesus. Here are some bitter root judgements that may have formed:
- My sister would order me around like she was my mother, but I needed a companion not another mom. Jesus isn't my companion.
- My brother was really mean to me, so Jesus must be like my brother.

The Holy Trinity is nothing like human beings yet the enemy gets you to put human traits on THEM that come from the way human beings have treated you. It's a really sly trick of the enemy against you and it's proven to be one of the best tools against humans he can use.

Healing begins with accepting responsibility for your own beliefs and judgments and not by blaming others for what happened/happens.

3. Four common characteristics of bitter root judgments:

   a. All things produce after their own kind. We reap what we sow. The seeds we sow multiply. Blessings naturally produce blessings. Curses produce curses. And _____ naturally produce more judgments.

b. The longer a judgment continues in a person's life, the more _____ takes hold. The seeds of judgment may seem tiny when you look back on your childhood experiences, but when you hold on to that judgment into your adulthood it can grow and multiply many times.

c. Bitter Root Judgments are like strong _____ in your life. Whatever judgments you have, you will be drawn to others who possess the same characteristics as your judgments. In this manner not only will your judgments be fulfilled, but they will also be strengthened. You bring to you what you give out.

Examples: All men are jerks, thus men will be jerks around you.

What you believe is most often what you will receive.

d. Bitter Root Judgments are like _____.

Symptoms of the Hatred/Rage Door that we open up to the enemy. Hatred is to love less than we should. Check any of these that apply to you:

- ❏ Resentment
- ❏ Bitterness
- ❏ Envy
- ❏ Gossip
- ❏ Pride
- ❏ Rage
- ❏ Wanting to get even or vengeance
- ❏ Records kept of wrongs
- ❏ Comparison
- ❏ Competition
- ❏ Jealousy
- ❏ Expectations of anyone (must give to THEM)
- ❏ Self hatred
- ❏ Self image
- ❏ Self protector
- ❏ Self sufficiency
- ❏ Self sabotage
- ❏ Self deception/self deceived
- ❏ Self centeredness
- ❏ Self awareness that is out of balance
- ❏ Selfishness
- ❏ OCD, ODD, ADHD, ADD and other labels

4. Forgiveness is always *the* key to _____. You need to forgive the individual involved when the bitter root attached. You will also need to seek forgiveness for the sin of making the judgment. Don't forget to give your records/account of wrongdoing to Jesus.

> *"But if you do not forgive men their sins, your Father will not forgive your sins."*
>
> **Matthew 6:15**

> *"And whenever you stand praying, if you find that you carry something in your heart against another person, release him and forgive him so that your Father in heaven will also release you and forgive you of your faults."*
>
> **Mark 11:25**

> *"So then, if you are presenting a gift before the altar in the temple and suddenly you remember a quarrel you have with a fellow believer, leave your gift there in front of the altar and go at once to apologize with the one who is offended. Then, after you have reconciled, come to the altar and present your gift."*
>
> **Matthew 5:23-24**

5. Let's go a bit deeper on the records you keep against someone else or yourself.
   a. These can be known records, that are easy to retrieve.
   b. These can be hidden records that you don't know are there, because you believe you have forgiven but you have held onto the record as a protection against future projected hurts from that person.

When true forgiveness is there, the incident that occurred holds no _____ over you and it is like the event that occurred actually happened to another person even though it happened to you.

The enemy's point of view is designed to take you and the person you hold a record against, captive. He will get you to believe a lie and get you to transfer that lie on to the Holy Trinity or even to believe that lie about yourself.

 Reminder: If you overreact to someone, it may be that you've been triggered. This isn't about their behavior. They may have unburied an old Bitter Root Judgement that you need to heal.

Every situation carries the intent of what the enemy wants to accomplish in you and there is the intent of Heaven for you. The question becomes whose intent are you coming into agreement with?

The intent of the enemy will bring unhappiness and illness into your life. John 10:10

> *"For I know the plans I have for you," declares the Lord, "plans to prosper you and not to harm you, plans to give you hope and a future."*
>
> **Jeremiah 29:11**

The intent of the Holy Trinity will bring you only happiness and goodness into your life. If what is going on in your life does not make you hopeful and give you a great future, then it is not what THEY want for you.

Keeping records against people is one of the enemy's strategies to use against you and yours. If you keep records that you constantly bring up then the enemy will make sure that your family learns to keep records on you too.

"So then, surrender to God. Stand up to the devil and resist him and he will turn and run away from you."

James 4:7

"THINK only on what is good, noble, just, praiseworthy..."

Philippians 4:8

In other words, if the thoughts I am having about humans will not live in HEAVEN-I need to choose another thought. This also works with my actions, emotions and attitudes. So let's take a look at a divided heart.

6. Faith responds with Who God said He is and what He has ALREADY done in the Person of Jesus Christ. This graphic really helped me understand how my past hurts can _____ my future.

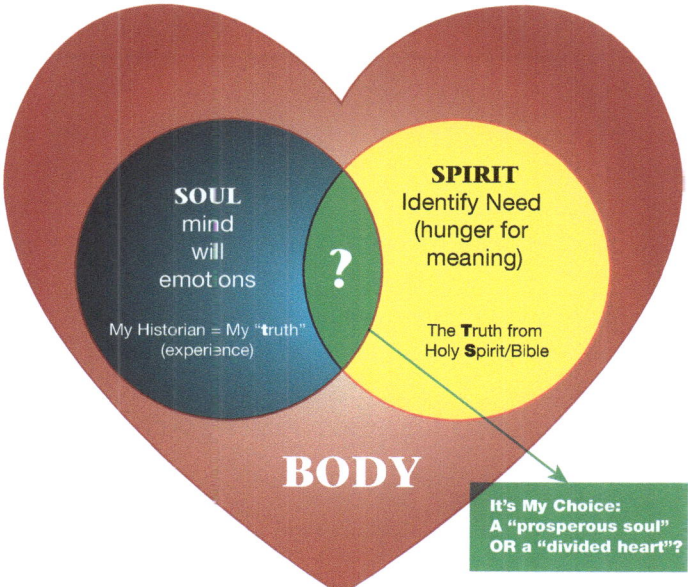

What you believe in your soul (mind, will, emotions) is largely based on your history. This includes your family's beliefs and values (including Family Imprints which we address in Lesson 4.) Doctrines or theology you were taught in church (and professed), your childhood and adult experiences, etc.—All of your history becomes the lens through which you see the present and it impacts how you view the future.

Changing your beliefs can be challenging because your default is to go back to your little "t" truth from your history. This is deeply engrained in your soul – your mind will and emotions – which becomes your mindset. A mindset by definition is a fixed mental attitude or disposition that predetermines a person's responses to and interpretations of situations, an inclination or a habit.

Adapted from A Prosperous Soul workshop by Stephen DeSilva, Zion Christian Fellowship, 2/24/18

Your mindset is a set of beliefs that shape how you make sense of the world and yourself. It influences how you think, feel and behave in any given situation. It's how you see the world. Carol Dweck is an authority on growth mindsets and she says,

> **❝ More and more research is suggesting that, far from being simply encoded in the genes, much of personality is a flexible and dynamic thing that changes over the lifespan and is shaped by experience. ❞**
> **Carol Dweck**

If you've never personally experienced physical healing and/or have rarely if ever seen anyone else healed – your history becomes your "truth" (little "t" truth). And satan reinforces that "truth" from your history by holding you captive through his lies.

This is in contrast to your spirit which thirsts and hungers for meaning and Kingdom identity from The "Truth" (capital "T" Truth) from Holy Spirit and the Bible. Could this be why there is such an emphasis in the Bible on transforming and renewing your mind?

And He has taught you to let go of the lifestyle of the ancient man, the old self-life, which was corrupted by sinful and deceitful desires that spring from delusions. Now it's time to be made new by every revelation that's been given to you. And to be transformed as you embrace the glorious Christ-within as your new life and live in union with Him! For God has re-created you all over again in His perfect righteousness, and you now belong to Him in the realm of true holiness.

Ephesians 4:22-24

I know that You delight to set Your Truth deep in my spirit. So come into the hidden places of my heart and teach me wisdom. Keep creating in me a clean heart. Fill me with pure thoughts and holy desires, ready to please You. Let my passion for life be restored; tasting joy in every breakthrough You bring to me. Hold me close to You with a willing spirit that obeys whatever You say.

Psalm 51:6, 10, 12

51:6 The Hebrew word bat-ṭuchâh, although difficult to translate, can mean "something that is covered over, hidden, or concealed." This could be paraphrased as "You desire light in my darkness" or "You want Truth to expose my secrets."
51:10 The word used for "create" takes us back to Gen. 1, and it means to create from nothing. David knew he had no goodness without God placing it within him. David wanted a new creation heart, not just the old one changed.
51:10 Or "Renew a reliable spirit in my inner being."

In your **soul** (your mind, will and emotions) is where your own "Historian" lives. Your historian keeps track of all the things you've done and said to remind you of who you are. It is your little "t" **t**ruth of your lived experiences. This is where shame, disappointment, and regret live because of what you've done in the past. It is often where the enemy will taunt you with what people said to you and about you which often are lies and they certainly don't line up with what God and His Scripture says about you (1).

In your **spirit** is your hunger for meaning and for identity. It is in your spirit that you receive the capital "T" **T**ruth from Holy Spirit who fills you as a believer and it's where Scripture declares who you are as a son/daughter of the King of Kings.

In the intersection between your soul and spirit is a question mark that is a CHOICE that you make each and every day. Will you believe and receive 3 John 2 (TPT) Prosperous Soul, *"Beloved friend, I pray that you are prospering in every way and that you continually enjoy good health, just as your soul is prospering"* When you have a prosperous soul, your body will be healthy according to that Scripture. Even good health begins in your soul, not your body.

The other choice you have in that intersection is Romans 7:15 (NIV) which is the Divided Heart, *"I do not understand what I do. For what I want to do I do not do, but what I hate I do."* It means you are believing the "history" of your past and that Jesus' death, burial, and resurrection was not enough to erase your sins.

Jesus not only forgives but He forgets your sins (Psalm 103:12). So then why do you keep reminding Him of those sins? Let it go. Focus on God's **T**ruth so you have a prosperous soul.

In the rest of this book you will examine your little "t" truth and history and pull out the lies and replace them with Biblical **T**ruth. Here's the reality: What you focus on (believe), you receive!

That's why it's so important that you are careful with your words (What I say) because words (e.g. decrees) determine your future (What I get). It's also critical that you don't receive and believe negative words that people speak over you (bitter root judgements) including from your childhood.

Isn't it time for you to let go of your past history and move into your future?

> *Now, if anyone is enfolded into Christ, he has become an entirely new person. All that is related to the old order has vanished. Behold, everything is fresh and new.*
> **2 Corinthians 5:17**

5:17 This would include our old identity, our life of sin, the power of Satan, the religious works of trying to please God, our old relationship with the world, and our old mind-

sets. We are not reformed or simply refurbished, we are made completely new by our union with Christ and the indwelling of the Holy Spirit.
5:17 Or "Behold, a new order has come!"

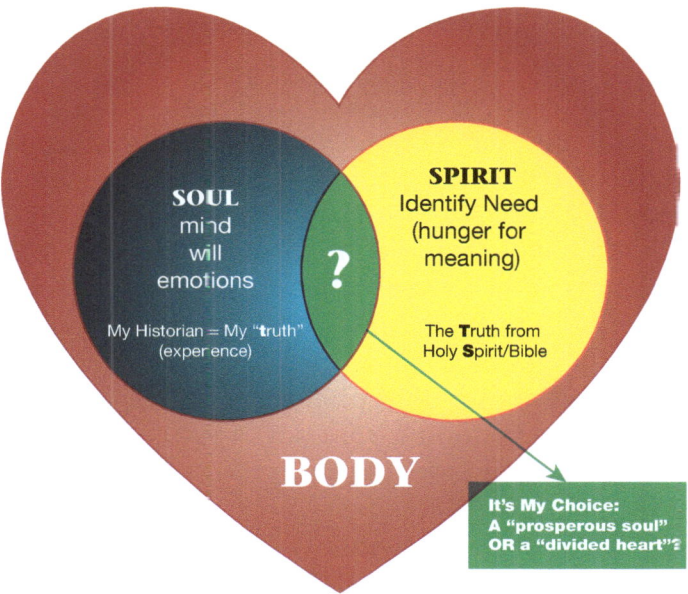

The Truth from the Bible clearly states you must transform your mindset to line up with what God says about you. You are a new creation. By His stripes you are healed.

> **He has plans to prosper you and not to harm you, plans to give you a hope and a future.**
>
> **Jeremiah 29:11**

Where the soul and spirit intersect shows the choice you need to make between a prosperous soul OR a divided heart (double mindedness). Your decision of which lens you view the world through will directly affect your body – for what I think, I believe and do; and what I say, my body will obey.

> **Prosperous Soul - Beloved friend, I pray that you are prospering in every way and that you continually enjoy good health, just as your soul is prospering.**
>
> **3 John 2**

> *Divided Heart - I do not understand what I do. For what I want to do I do not do, but what I hate I do.*
>
> **Romans 7:15 (NIV)**

Once again, you must pull out the lies you believe and replace it with Biblical Truth (what God says). For me, I had to really examine my core theology/doctrine. My church didn't teach about Holy Spirit, Pentecost or healing. Were those things absent from the Bible? Did that absence prevent me from experiencing divine health and or seeing people healed in the name of Jesus?

It's important to recognize that often your soul is ferocious in protecting your history including your doctrine and personal experience. It's what we call a besetting sin.

> *As for us, we have all of these great witnesses who encircle us like clouds. So we must **let go of every wound** that has pierced us and the sin we so easily fall into (besetting sin). Then we will be able to run life's marathon race with passion and determination, for the path has been already marked out before us.*
>
> **Hebrews 12:1**

Isn't it time to let go of old, worn out beliefs that aren't Biblical and don't serve you well?

Here's an exercise to replace truth with God's Truth so you can get rid of your bad fruit that is coming from the roots of your thoughts (mindset) which is based in the seed of your trauma and wounds.

Inner Healing Process with Wrong Beliefs/Lies:

Say: *In the name of Jesus Christ I confess that I have believed the lie:*_____. Place the pain/loss this lie has cost you in your hands. The pain this lie has caused me is_____. Are you ready to give all of this pain and grief to Jesus and be done with it? Then say: *I release to you Jesus all my pain (tell Him what pain)*_____. *I ask you Jesus, to forgive me for believing this lie. I break the power of this lie____(lie)____in the name of Jesus Christ and I sever it with the Sword of the Spirit. I renounce any demonization that exists as a result of this lie. Holy Spirit, what will You give me in exchange for my lie/pain?*_____. (Give person time to hear from God). Do you receive that from Him? *Holy Spirit, what is the Truth from Your Word instead of my lie?*_____. *I turn my back on this lie and choose instead to believe____(the truth)____and I can walk it out in Jesus Christ. Amen!*

7. One of the blessings that come with breaking inner vows and Bitter Root Judgments is that the cycle is _____. Changes will take place. Sometimes the changes will be subtle, and at other times more dramatic.

   a. As your beliefs are conformed to God's Word by the _____ of your mind, the things that use to bother and irritate you will now _____ of you.

   b. As your beliefs are turned from deception to _____, you are one step closer to being conformed into the image of your Lord Jesus Christ and producing the fruit of the Spirit.

What Bitter Root Judgments are you willing to break in order to renew your mind and grow in the fruit of the Spirit?

_____

_____

_____

_____

_____

_____

_____

_____

Examples of Common Bitter Root Judgements that lead to Unhealthy Patterns/Fruit:

Note that Bitter Root Judgments are absolutes. It's either all or nothing. There's very little room for grace, mercy, and forgiveness. Some common Bitter Root Judgments are:

❏ Others are to make me happy.
❏ No one respects me.
❏ If I tell the truth people will be angry with me.
❏ No one trusts me.
❏ No one ever wants to hear what I have to say.
❏ No one really cares…
❏ People in authority will hurt you (or take advantage of you).
❏ All women (or men) are controlling.
❏ God doesn't hear me.
❏ Men (or women) only want one thing.
❏ No one needs me.
❏ If you give someone an inch they'll take a mile.
❏ God doesn't care.
❏ No one likes me (wants to be my friend).
❏ Others see my sin (or shame).
❏ Everyone thinks I'm stupid.
❏ Everyone thinks I'm ugly.
❏ Friends never remain faithful.
❏ Others always end up rejecting me.
❏ Others won't allow me in.
❏ Everyone looks down on me.
❏ Relationships never last.
❏ Everyone lies.
❏ People (and God) won't forgive me.
❏ Everyone else gets the breaks.
❏ Others don't see my worth (value).
❏ White people can't dance.
❏ If I share my heart it will be broken.
❏ All Christians are hypocrites.
❏ No one sees my loneliness.
❏ You're never satisfied.
❏ No one will ever love me again.
❏ Everyone sees my confusion.

8. How to break Bitter Root Judgments
   a. Identify the event or person in your life that caused you to make the Bitter Root Judgment. Go back to the first time you recall thinking/making your judgment.
   b. Go through the healing process of the event/events that brought you to make the judgment by recalling and then releasing your pain to Jesus.
   c. Choose to forgive the person/people involved. Give your records/account of wrongdoing to Jesus.
   d. Ask God to forgive you for passing the judgments.
   e. Sever the judgment with the Sword of the Spirit.
   f. Confess the Bitter Root Judgment and break its hold in the name of Jesus Christ.
   g. Choose to believe the Truth that God gave you in exchange.
   h. Pronounce a blessing on the offender.
      Romans 12:14 says to "Bless those who persecute you; bless and do not curse."

Select a Bitter Root Judgment that impacts your life that you want to deal with:

_____

_____

_____

_____

_____

_____

_____

_____

_____

_____

_____

_____

_____

_____

_____

_____

_____

Hiding Place Activation

Sit quietly in a comfortable position. Close your eyes the entire time in a posture of prayer. Remember there will be a lot of quiet time during this activation so just relax in His Presence.

Take several deep breaths, letting them out slowly. Again breathe in, breathe out.

Here are some verses related to bitter root judgments to read out loud:

"Do not be deceived. God is not mocked, for whatever a man sows, this he will also reap."   Galatians 6:7

"Do not judge or you too will be judged. For in the same way you judge others, you will be judged, and with the measure you use, it will be measured to you."   Matthew 7:1-2

"So then, if you are presenting a gift before the altar in the temple and suddenly you remember a quarrel you have with a fellow believer, leave your gift there in front of the altar and go at once to apologize with the one who is offended. Then, after you have reconciled, come to the altar and present your gift." Matthew 5:23-24

Watch your words and be careful what you say, and you'll be surprised how few troubles you'll have.   Proverbs 21: 23

First, you're going to pray Psalm 31: 20 over yourself:
20 So hide me Your beloved one in the sheltered, secret hiding place before Your face. Overshadow me by Your glory-presence…Tuck me safely away in the tabernacle where You dwell.

Lord, I want You to take me back to Our hiding place now. Go back with Him to your hiding place. Then rest in His Presence and love for as long as you like.

Praying Scripture Prior to Healing Bitter Root Judgments:

Pray from Psalm 139:23-24 TPT. Say out loud: "God, I invite Your searching gaze into my heart. Examine me through and through; find out everything that may be hidden within me. Put me to the test and sift through all my anxious cares. See if there is any path of pain I'm walking on, and lead me back to Your glorious, ever-lasting ways— the path that brings me back to You."

Now, you're going to invite Holy Spirit to bring you back to your bitter root judgment:

Before we do the healing prayer, I want you to say: *Holy Spirit, please show me the pain that this Bitter Root Judgment has cost me in my life.*

_____

_____

_____

_____

Holy Spirit, what records/account of wrongdoing have I been holding on to?

_____

_____

_____

Holy Spirit, show me if I am suffering from any physical, emotional, or mental disease due to my bitter root judgments?

_____

_____

_____

_____

Sample Healing Prayer

In the name of Jesus Christ I confess I have carried (hold in your hands) *the Bitter Root Judgment of* _____(judgment)_____. *I release my pain of* _____(specify the pain)_____ *and give it to You* (hand it up to Him), *Jesus. I also give You my records/ account of wrongdoings* (hand Him the papers) *from my bitter root judgment. What will You do with these records?* Write down what you see/feel/ hear: _____ .

Jesus, what will You give me in exchange for that pain and my records? Write it down.

_____

_____

_____

Thank You Jesus, I receive that. I forgive (wipe your hands) _____ (name)_____ *for the way they treated me. In Jesus Christ's name, I command* (salute) *complete healing and restoration of* _____(disease)____ (point to heaven then to you) *caused by my bitter root judgment. By Your stripes* (touch nail holes) *I am healed. Thank you Jesus.*

Please Jesus forgive me for my judgment. I break (clap) *the power of the Bitter Root Judgment of* _____(judgment)_____ *in my life. In the name of Jesus Christ, I sever* (cut it) *the judgment with the Sword of the Spirit. I turn my back* (turn around) *on this judgment. I renounce any demonization* (cross your arms) *that exists as a result of my judgment. Jesus, what is Your Truth* (point up) *about my Bitter Root Judgement?*__ (the Truth)_____ *I choose now to believe* _____(the Truth)_____ . *I ask a blessing* (reach out to them) *on* _____(name)_____ *who hurt and offended me.*

I commit (clasp hands) *this day to walk out my healing with Jesus' help by His blood* (touch crucifixion nail holes) *and in His* (point up) *powerful name*: Clap!

_____<signature>_____<date>_____ .

Homework This Week

1. Say out loud this week's Breakthrough Decrees daily.

2. Share with a friend the Bitter Root Judgment that most negatively impacted your life, the Truth you received from Jesus, and what steps you are taking to walk in victory. Share one way they can support you in your healing journey with bitter root judgments.

3. New Habit: Pray <u>for</u> your enemy (read Matthew 5:43-48).

4. Join us on our Mentoring Call.

5. Write in your Victory and Gratitude Journals.

Daily Gratitude Journal

Write down 3 things you are thankful or grateful for each day.

Date:_____1. _____

2. _____

3. _____

Date:_____1. _____

2. _____

3. _____

Date:_____1. _____

2. _____

3. _____

Date:_____1. _____

2. _____

3. _____

Date:_____1. _____

2. _____

3. _____

Date:_____1. _____

2. _____

3. _____

Date:_____1. _____

2. _____

3. _____

Date:_____1. _____

2. _____

3. _____

Date:_____1. _____

2. _____

3. _____

Breakthrough Decrees (repeat daily)
(activate your words with body action)

1. I sow good seeds and attract positive people to my life. (Galatians 6:7).

2. I am not easily offended (Matthew 7:1-2; Hebrews 2:15).

3. I forgive others quickly and what used to bother me rolls off easily (Mark 11:25).

4. I think and believe the best of others (Philippians 2:3; 4:8).

5. I will bless others and not curse them. I speak words of encouragement to others (1 Corinthians 13:7 and Romans 12:14).

   On this day _____, I establish these decrees that are founded in God's Word.

   Signed: _____

Victory Journal of Your Progress

Check any of the Bitter Root Judgments that apply to you (on page 144). Pray for the Holy Spirit to identify any other Bitter Root Judgments in your life (that may not be on the list). Pray through the steps of breaking each of those judgments.

You may want to make a list of your judgments as well as the Truth as a reminder to you:

My Bitter Root Judgments: The Truth:

_____   _____
_____   _____
_____   _____
_____   _____
_____   _____
_____   _____
_____   _____
_____   _____
_____   _____
_____   _____
_____   _____
_____   _____
_____   _____
_____   _____
_____   _____
_____   _____
_____   _____
_____   _____
_____   _____
_____   _____
_____   _____

Use additional pages if you need more room.

Fill-in-the-Blank Answer Guide

1. others   me
    a. stronghold
    b. bitterness
3. a. judgments
    b. bitterness
    c. magnets
    d. lassos
4. healing
5. impact
6. limit
7. broken
    a. renewing   roll off
    b. Truth

Personal Notes

_____

_____

_____

_____

_____

_____

_____

_____

_____

_____

_____

_____

_____

_____

Resources

(1) Stephen Di Silva, A Prosperous Soul workshop, Zion Christian Fellowship, 2/24/18

When Others Curse You Intentionally or Unintentionally

> *"May those who bless you be blessed and those who curse you be cursed!"*
>
> **Numbers 24:9b**

> *"but the tongue is not able to be tamed. It's a fickle, unrestrained evil that spews out words full of toxic poison! We use our tongue to praise God our Father and then turn around and curse a person who was made in His very image! Out of the same mouth we pour out words of praise one minute and curses the next. My brothers and sister, this should never be!"*
>
> **James 3:8-10**

You know from the Bible that there is power in the tongue—life and death are in your words. This lesson is written to help you break the curses that have been spoken over you (intentionally or unintentionally) or that you have spoken over others.

Your life can be negatively impacted by your own family if someone is not welcomed into the family. While my parents gave Jim their blessing to ask for my hand in marriage, my mother did not accept Jim as my husband. Her expectations of marriage were different than mine. I delayed our marriage by six months as a result of the chaos my mom sowed by intruding in our relationship. She unintentionally cursed our marriage.

You unknowingly may curse other people and your relationships by talking with friends about your struggles. Our words are <u>very</u> powerful and can be prophetic seeds. By definition prophetic means: *accurately describing or predicting what will happen in the future*. Please understand that the word "sarcasm" in Greek means "tear flesh" so don't ever say, "I was just kidding when I said that." You just tore another person's flesh. There's nothing joking or kidding about sarcasm so stop it now!

Are you speaking encouraging words that build up or curse words that tear down others and your relationships?

> *"⁷God will never be mocked! For what you plant will always be the very thing you harvest. ⁸The harvest you reap reveals the seed that you planted. If you plant the corrupt seeds of self-life into this natural realm, you can expect a harvest of corruption. If you plant the good seeds of Spirit life you will reap beautiful fruits that grow from the everlasting life of the Spirit.*
>
> *⁹And don't allow yourselves to be weary in planting good seeds, for the season of reaping the wonderful harvest you've planted is coming!*
>
> *¹⁰Take advantage of every opportunity to be a blessing to others, especially to our brothers and sisters in the family of faith!"*
>
> **Galatians 6:7-9**

> *"God, give me grace to guard my lips from speaking what is wrong."*
>
> **Psalm 141: 3**

What a lesson I learned firsthand about the power of unintentional curses with my son Bryan. At the end of this lesson, I will tell you the "rest of the story" about Bryan. Nationwide research indicates that about 20% of students ages 12-18 experience bullying. Bullying affects all youth, including those who are bullied, those who bully others, and those who witness bullying. The effects of bullying may continue into adulthood.

Bullying is a form of cursing others and it results in hurts that live on into adulthood. It changes one's belief system. If you receive what others say about you as a child into your soul (your mind, will, emotions), you'll walk it out in your life unless you learn how to break those curses (which hurt you). That is what we talk about in this lesson.

Another form of bullying is cancel culture which became a common term in 2020. Cancel culture is when people decide they don't like what someone said or did, and they try to punish that person by making others not like them too. It began as a way to stand up against powerful people, but now it's being used for pretty much everybody.

#CancelCulture

Cancel culture is like bullying in that it's mean and doesn't give a person an opportunity to learn. Instead of helping people understand each other better, cancelling just pushes people away. It's important to find a way to talk about problems and to give people a chance to express opinions. (1)

Many family relationships have changed as a result of covid19 where families pit themselves against each other and isolated from one another. What we experienced was satan at work stealing, killing, destroying and dividing us through covid.

> *The thief comes only to steal and kill and destroy; I have come that they may have life, and have it to the full.*
> **John 10:10 NIV**

During the Covid-19 pandemic, depression and anxiety in youth doubled compared to pre-pandemic levels, according to research. One in 4 adolescents globally are "experiencing clinically elevated depression symptoms, while 1 in 5 youth are experiencing clinically elevated anxiety symptoms." "Results from this analysis suggest that the pandemic has likely instigated a global mental health crisis in youth," said study author Sheri Madigan. (2) The enemy is after our children!

1. To curse is primarily an Old Testament concept. It is a
   _____ _____ meant to release negative spiritual power against the object, person, or place being cursed.
   a. Three times God declares He will curse the one who curses His people. Read Numbers 24:9.
   b. Noah pronounced a curse on Canaan and a blessing on Shem and Japheth (Genesis 9:25-27)
   c. Isaac blesses his twin sons and pronounces a curse upon anyone who would want to curse Jacob. (Genesis 27)

The power released in either blessing or cursing was considered _____. The curse was to be feared and the blessing to be coveted.

2. Current day curses may be pronounced by:
    a. Someone who continues to speak _____words over you or about you. For instance, "You are stupid". The more it is said, it takes on a stronghold over your soul.

    b. Intercessors may _____ pray and actually speak a curse over someone. For example, praying that God would burn down the porno store instead of praying for redemption.

    c. A person claiming someone as his or her spouse when there is no mutual interest is pronouncing a curse of _____ on that person.

    d. Can Christians curse other Christians? _____.

To curse a man is to curse God (see James 3:9 as man is made in God's image)

> *"With the tongue we praise our Lord and Father, and with it we curse men, who have been made in God's likeness."*
>
> **James 3:9 (NIV)**

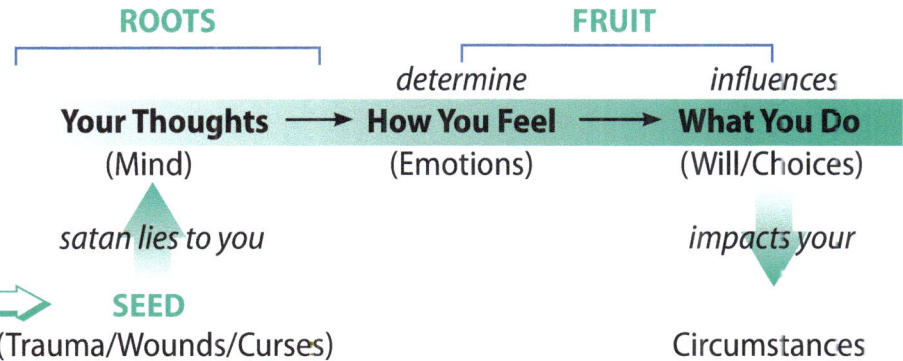

ROOTS   **FRUIT**

determine   *influences*

Your Thoughts ⟶ **How You Feel** ⟶ **What You Do**

(Mind) (Emotions) (Will/Choices)

satan lies to you   *impacts your*

SEED

(Trauma/Wounds/Curses)   Circumstances

The 1828 Webster's Dictionary defines curse as "To utter a wish of evil against another. To inflict or torment or bring condemnation."

T. Lewis and R.K. Harrison (in *The Handbook for Spiritual Warfare* by Dr. Ed Murphy,) informs us: *"When a curse is pronounced against any person we are not to understand this as a mere wish, however violent, that disaster should overtake the person in question any more than we are to understand that a corresponding "blessing" conveys simply a wish that prosperity should be the lot of the person on whom the blessing is involved. A curse was considered to possess an inherent power for carrying itself into effect ... Such curses (and Blessings) possess power."*

3. God has called us to be a people of _____. Wisdom tells us to pay attention to curses sent or spoken over us. They can take on a demonic power that will hinder one from moving in _____.

4. Holiness is a key to our protection. In Numbers 23, Balak used divination to send curses to Israel. But, Balak did not understand that the _____ of a person is a means of protection against evil. What Balam told Balak there was no gate or opportunity for the curses he sent to take root.

> *"He has not observed iniquity in Jacob, nor has He seen wickedness in Israel. The LORD his God is with him, and the shout of a King is among them. God brings them out of Egypt; He has strength like a wild ox. For there is no sorcery against Jacob, nor any divination against Israel. It now must be said of Jacob and of Israel, 'Oh, what God has done!'"*
>
> **Numbers 23:21-23** (NKJV)

5. Who might possibly curse or intentionally hurt you?

    a. Curses from religious cult groups: Some religious cult groups pray multiple times each day. Those prayers stir the heavens of oppression—words have power that can release the forces of _____.

We are in a spiritual _____ so be prepared to pray daily against those prayers of false religions who declare that we are their enemies. You may want to pray "In the name and blood of Jesus Christ, I cancel every curse sent over me by ungodly prayers."

b. Curses from the occult

> *"Then Pharaoh also called the wise men and sorcerers: now the magicians of Egypt, they also did in like manner with their enchantments."*
>
> **Exodus 7:11**

- These "wise men" are people whose practical advice is based upon _____ revelation (see Jeremiah 50:35; Ezekiel 27:9, Obadiah 8).
  These "wise men" practiced magic and divination. Their revelation was from other gods instead of the true God of Israel.
- The word "sorcerer" comes from the Hebrew word *kashaph* which means "to whisper a _____ _____; to use songs of magic; to mutter magical words of incantations; to enchant; to practice magic; to be a sorcerer; to use witchcraft. They were known to have power from evil spirits.
- "Magician" is from the Hebrew word *chartom*. Here it means Egyptian or Babylonian sages and magicians who practiced the _____, sorcery, and incantations.
- The Hebrew word for "enchantment" is *lahat*. It means something covered up by the use of secret arts and _____.

As we understand the meaning of the above words, it will help us understand the significance of the occult practices today. There is nothing new under the sun.

Personal Self-Assessment

Symptoms of the Door of the Occult that we open up to the enemy. Please check any of these that you've been involved in or even dabbled in.

- ❏ Spiritism
- ❏ Magic
- ❏ Palm Reading
- ❏ Fortune Tellers
- ❏ Horoscopes
- ❏ Tarot cards
- ❏ Ouija Board
- ❏ Hypnosis
- ❏ Yoga
- ❏ Anything that is dark, dark TV shows, dark movies, dark books, dark video games, Twilight series, Harry Potter, Vampires
- ❏ Free Masonry
- ❏ Drugs
- ❏ Judgement
- ❏ Criticism
- ❏ Control
- ❏ Manipulation
- ❏ Idols anything that is bigger than God

c. Unintentional "friendly-fire" curses include:
- • Personal curses of oppression—curses sent over our:
  Body/Health—spoken by health care professionals
  Finances
  Marriage—spoken to each other
- • Curses from _____ figures including parents, teachers, pastors, etc.
- • Curses in the _____ – gossip, prayer

d. Family Imprints (see Lesson 4)

These words have a _____ _____ on the soul and can become strongholds that prevent a person from believing in him/herself.

What unintentional word curses have you said about your family or other people (and shared with others)?

_____

_____

6. When Moses went to Pharaoh to see the release of the Israelites, he went under the _____ of God. There were several curses that the magicians could perform, but they finally gave up and said Moses must be sent from God.

   The great news for all believers is that the curses against them could not bring _____ to God's people.

> *"For our struggle is not against flesh and blood, but against the rulers, against the authorities, against the powers of this dark world and against the spiritual forces of evil in the heavenly realms."*
>
> **Ephesians 6:12**

7. What are the symptoms of being cursed?

   a. Oppression is the main one. It is a _____ that seems to be surrounding you.

   b. _____ can be caused by curses in particular areas such as heart attacks, back pain, headaches, etc.

   c. Curses may be sent over your _____ . What better way to limit the influence of the church than to limit the money coming into the church through tithes and offerings.

   d. Curses may be sent to Christian families to destroy the _____ of the leaders.

e. Curses are sent upon the _____ and areas specifically where there are churches working toward reconciliation
between races. Satan wants division not unity. Example:
Tecumseh and Chillicothe

8. How to Break Curses Sent by Others:

First, You need to understand the Power of the Cross. Only when
you understand the cross do you understand the power of the Blood.
Placing the cross in prayer between you and an area of sin is a type
of symbolic or visual prayer. If the cross is between you and the sin,
then you have to go back through the cross to pick the sin up again.

> *"Christ redeemed us from that self-defeating, cursed life
> by absorbing it completely into Himself. Do you remember
> the Scripture that says, "Cursed is everyone who hangs
> on a tree"? That is what happened when Jesus was nailed
> to the cross: He became a curse, and at the same time
> dissolved the curse."*
>
> **Galatians 3:13 The Message**

Second, pronounce in the Name of Jesus Christ that the curse be
broken. Be sure to speak the curse by name.

Third, command all that had been taken by the enemy to be
restored, plus sevenfold more.

> *"Yet if he (the thief) is caught, he must pay sevenfold
> though it costs him all the wealth of his house."*
>
> **Proverbs 6:31**

Fourth, forgive the person who sent the curse. You do not need
to know who sent the curse, just pronounce forgiveness. If the
curse has taken a strong root in you, then you need to spend time
with the Lord to find out what sin in your life has allowed the
curse to become a stronghold. Seek forgiveness and choose not to
walk in whatever area of sin God may reveal.

Fifth, seal the healing with the Blood of Jesus Christ.

 **Personal Application/Exercise**

1. Is there any problem areas that I am dealing with in my relationships that could be the result of a curse? Then pray about that area and ask the Holy Spirit to reveal if this is actually a curse.

    _____

    _____

    _____

2. Any records/accounts of wrongdoing that I need to give to Jesus?

    _____

    _____

    _____

3. Do I need to seek forgiveness for any curses I may have placed on my family or others?

    _____

    _____

    _____

4. Ask God to reveal to you any curse that has been placed on the land where you live. If there is a curse, break it and ask God to bring forth His blessings upon the land.

    _____

    _____

    _____

Hiding Place Activation

Sit quietly in a comfortable position. Close your eyes the entire time in a posture of prayer. Remember there will be a lot of quiet time during this activation so just relax in His Presence.

Take several deep breaths, letting them out slowly. Again breathe in, breathe out.

Here are some verses related to curses to read out loud:

> *"but the tongue is not able to be tamed. It's a fickle, unrestrained evil that spews out words full of toxic poison! We use our tongue to praise God our Father and then turn around and curse a person who was made in His very image! Out of the same mouth we pour out words of praise one minute and curses the next. My brothers and sister, this should never be!*
>
> **James 3:8-10**
>
> *"May those who bless you be blessed and those who curse you be cursed!"*
>
> **Numbers 24:9b**
>
> *"As a man thinks in his heart so he is."*
>
> **Proverbs 27:7**

First, you're going to pray Psalm 31: 20 over yourself:
20 So hide me Your beloved one in the sheltered, secret hiding place before Your face. Overshadow me by Your glory-presence...Tuck me safely away in the tabernacle where You dwell. Lord, I want You to take me back to our hiding place now. Go back with Him to your hiding place. Then rest in His Presence and love for as long as you like.

Praying Scripture Prior to Breaking the Curse(s):
Pray from Psalm 139:23-24 TPT. Say out loud: *"God, I invite Your searching gaze into my heart. Examine me through and through; find out everything that may be hidden within me. Put me to the test and sift through all my anxious cares. See if there is any path of pain I'm walking on, and lead me back to Your glorious, everlasting ways— the path that brings me back to You."*

In the exercises above, you may have identified several curses that you need to break. Select and deal with one curse at a time.

Now, you're going to invite Jesus to bring you back to your curse situation by asking Jesus: *Jesus, show me the earliest situation where I was cursed* _____(curse)_____. Write down what you see/hear/feel/know.

_____

_____

_____

_____

Ask Jesus: *What pain has this caused me in my life?*

_____

_____

_____

_____

Show me if I am suffering from any physical or emotional disease due to curses spoken over me?

_____

_____

_____

_____

Sample Healing Prayer to Break a Curse Over You

In Jesus Christ's name, I break the power of any curse of _____(curse)_____ *that has been spoken against me. I cancel* (slash) *the assignment of those words/curses. I release the pain* (give it to Jesus) *to you Jesus that this curse has caused me* _____(pain)_____ . *I forgive* (wipe your hands) _____(name)_____ *for cursing me. I also give You the records/account* (hand over to Jesus) *that I've held about this curse. What do You want to do with these records Jesus?*

_____

What will You give me in exchange for my pain and records?

_____

Write down what you see/hear/feel.

_____

_____

_____

Thank You Jesus. I receive that (put hands out). *In Jesus Christ's name, I command* (salute) *complete healing and restoration* (point to heaven and then to you) *of* _____(disease)_____ *caused by this curse. By Your stripes* (touch the holes) *I am healed. Thank you Jesus. I commit* (clasp hands) *this day to walk out my healing with Jesus' help by His blood* (touch crucifixion nail holes) *and in His* (point up) *powerful name*: Clap!

_____<signature>_____<date>_____.

Sample Healing Prayer to Break Curse I Spoke

In Jesus Christ's name, I repent of and ask forgiveness for the curse I spoke _____(curse and person's name)_____. *I break* (sever it) *the power of that curse and cancel* (shake head no) *the assignment of my words in Jesus' name. In Jesus Christ's name and by His blood* (touch the holes), *I command* (point to heaven and then to the person) *complete restoration and healing of any pain or injury that I may have caused by this curse. I set* _____(person)_____ *free and I am free* (jump up in the victory stance) *from any bondage caused by that curse. I pray a blessing over* _____(name)_____.*God, give me grace to guard my lips from speaking what is wrong (Psalm 141:3).*

I commit (clasp hands) *this day to walk out my commitment with Jesus' help by His blood* (touch crucifixion nail holes) *and in His* (point up) *powerful name*: Clap!

_____<signature>_____   ____<date>_____.

> "**¹⁰Now my beloved ones, I have saved these most important truths for last: Be supernaturally infused with strength through your life-union with the Lord Jesus. Stand victorious with the force[a] of His explosive power flowing in and through you.**
>
> **¹¹ Put on God's complete set of armor provided for us, so that you will be protected as you fight against the evil strategies of the accuser!**
>
> **¹²Your hand-to-hand combat is not with human beings, but with the highest principalities and authorities operating in rebellion under the heavenly realms. For they are a powerful class of demon gods and evil spirits that hold this dark world in bondage.**
>
> **¹³Because of this, you must wear all the armor that God provides so you're protected as you confront the slanderer, for you are destined for all things and will rise victorious.**
>
> **¹⁴Put on truth as a belt to strengthen you to stand in triumph. Put on holiness as the protective armor that covers your heart.**
>
> **¹⁵Stand on your feet alert, then you'll always be ready to share the blessings of peace.**
>
> **¹⁶In every battle, take faith as your wrap around shield, for it is able to extinguish the blazing arrows coming at you from the Evil One.**
>
> **¹⁷⁻¹⁸Embrace the power of salvation's full deliverance, like a helmet to protect your thoughts from lies. And take the mighty razor-sharp Spirit sword of the spoken Word of God. Pray passionately in the Spirit, as you constantly intercede with every form of prayer at all times. Pray the blessings of God upon all His believers."**
>
> **Ephesians 6:10-18**

9. Exposing the _____ of the devil weakens him while at the same time empowering the believer for _____ . We can do nothing with our heads buried in the sand of apathy. Or, we can take our positions in God's army ready to move into battle.

We can hold back the darkness by walking more boldly in the light on a daily basis. Commit to becoming an active warrior in battling the forces of darkness against your family, your community, this nation, and the world.

> *"And the Lord shall make you the head, and not the tail; and you shall be above only, and you shall not be beneath, if you heed the commandments of the Lord your God which I command you this day and are watchful to do them."*
>
> **Deuteronomy 28:13** (The Message)

Homework This Week

1. Say out loud this week's Breakthrough Decrees daily.

2. Share with a friend the curse that most negatively impacted your life, the Truth you received from Jesus, and what steps you are taking to walk in victory. Share one way they can support you in your healing journey with soul ties. Ask for your friend to pray for you and then you pray for your friend.

3. New Habit: Check out the *Holy Bible You Version* cell phone app. Pick out a devotional that appeals to you. Connect with other friends on the app and see what they are reading and ways you can encourage one another. Consider downloading (free) The Passion Translation to inspire you with a new way of reading the Bible.

4. Read out loud to a friend the Renouncement of any family imprints to Free Masonry in the back of the book (takes 30-45 minutes).

5. Join us on our Mentoring Call.

6. Write in your Victory and Gratitude Journals.

Breakthrough Decrees (repeat daily)
(activate your words with body action)

1. When I'm upset or hurt, I do not react with anger (Matthew 5:21-22).

2. As I speak God's promises over my life, they come to pass. They stop all attacks, assaults, oppression, and fear from my life (2 Peter 1:2-4; Mark 11:23-24).

3. Any adversity, attack, accidents and tragedies that were headed my way are diverted right now in Jesus' name (Psalm 91).

4. Now I speak to every mountain of fear, every mountain of discouragement, every mountain of stress, every mountain of depression, every mountain of lack and insufficiency; and I say, "Be removed & cast into the sea in Jesus name!" (Mark 11:22-24).

5. I live under a supernatural protection (Psalm 91).

6. My truth to replace the lie:_____
   On this day _____, I establish these decrees that are founded in God's Word.

   Signed: _____

Some declarations used with permission of Steve and Wendy Backlund with IgnitingHope.com

Resources

The Handbook for Spiritual Warfare, Dr. Ed Murphy, Thomas Nelson Publishers, 1992.

(1) Cancel Culture: Accountability or Bullying? What do we teach kids when we condone public shaming? Psychology Today, Pamela B. Rutledge Ph.D., M.B.A. March 3, 2021

(2) Youth depression and anxiety doubled during the pandemic, new analysis finds. Sarah Molano, CNN Health. August 10, 2021

Victory Journal of Your Progress

You may want to make a list of the curses you have broken over yourself as well as the curses you have broken that you have spoken over others. This will serve as a reminder to your inner healing progress:

Others' Curses Over Me
I Have Broken: _____

Curses I Have Broken
Over Others: _____

_____   _____
_____   _____
_____   _____
_____   _____
_____   _____
_____   _____
_____   _____
_____   _____
_____   _____
_____   _____

Use additional pages if you need more room.

 **Your Victory Journal**

Write down what victories/wins you experienced this week.

_____
_____
_____
_____
_____
_____
_____
_____
_____
_____
_____
_____
_____
_____
_____
_____
_____
_____
_____
_____
_____
_____
_____
_____
_____
_____
_____
_____
_____

Daily Gratitude Journal

Write down 3 things you are thankful or grateful for each day.

Date:_____ 1. _____
2. _____
3. _____

Date:_____ 1. _____
2. _____
3. _____

Date:_____ 1. _____
2. _____
3. _____

Date:_____ 1. _____
2. _____
3. _____

Date:_____ 1. _____
2. _____
3. _____

Date:_____ 1. _____
2. _____
3. _____

Date:_____ 1. _____
2. _____
3. _____

Date:_____ 1. _____
2. _____
3. _____

Date:_____ 1. _____
2. _____
3. _____

1. power concept
   real
2. a. negative
   b. incorrectly
   c. bondage
   d. yes
3. prayer
   destiny
4. righteousness
5. a. evil   battle
   b. divination
      magic spell
      occult
      tricks
   c. authority
      church
   demonic power
6. anointing
   defeat
7. a. heaviness
   b. sickness
   c. finances
   d. children
   e. land
9. schemes
   battle

Resource: Bullying Research from: https://www.stopbullying.gov/resources/facts

Breaking Unhealthy Soul Ties

"One final word, friends. We ask you—urge is more like it—that you keep on doing what we told you to do to please God, not in a dogged religious plod, but in a living, spirited dance. You know the guidelines we laid out for you from the Master Jesus. God wants you to live a pure life. Keep yourselves from sexual promiscuity. Learn to appreciate and give dignity to your body, not abusing it, as is so common among those who know nothing of God. Don't run roughshod over the concerns of your brothers and sisters. Their concerns are God's concerns, and He will take care of them. We've warned you about this before. God hasn't invited us into a disorderly, unkempt life but into something holy and beautiful—as beautiful on the inside as the outside."

I Thessalonians 4:3-7 (The Message)

S oul ties are emotional bonds that form an attachment. They may be godly or ungodly, pure or demonic. Most people use the term soul tie to refer to connections linking people. Soul ties are not necessarily sexual or romantic. We can form an ungodly attachment with any person, place, or thing. Individuals can be overly attached to pets, possessions, or anything else imaginable:

Unhealthy soul ties can damage your relationships and inhibit your relationship with your potential spouse if you get married. It's like having an intruder enter your house. A soul tie with someone can destroy the trust and safety when you get married because that tie intrudes in your soul (your mind, will, and emotions). It's difficult to have oneness in marriage because you have more than two in your relationship. Soul ties need to be with only the mate God has created for you.

> *"...You are a slave to whatever controls you"*
> **2 Peter 2:19** (NLT)
>
> *"They traded the truth about God for a lie. So they worshiped and served the things God created instead of the Creator Himself, Who is worthy of eternal praise!"*
> **Romans 1:25** (NLT)

God doesn't want your soul in bondage to soul ties that turn your heart away from Him. God desires to restore your soul that you might be able to seek Him with your whole (entire) spirit, soul, and body.... You cannot be obedient to God's command to serve Him with all of your soul if you lack possession of a complete, whole soul! Let's begin this lesson with sexual soul ties.

> *"Now may the God of peace Himself sanctify you completely; and may your whole spirit, soul, and body be preserved blameless at the coming of our Lord Jesus Christ"*
> **1 Thessalonians 5:23**

1. God created you from the very beginning as _____ and _____. He intricately designed you as different genders in order to bring about the beauty of _____ through the blessing of sexual intercourse in marriage.

2. You cannot become loving human beings by simply being conceived and born. A person must be nurtured into the ability to truly _____ another person.

   a. The father's role is to _____ that life.

   b. The mother's role is to _____ that life.

   c. Some people who are involved in sex outside of marriage hate or strongly _____ their parents. They use sex as a subconscious way to throw away their parents' rights to rejoice in the child's glory. Women sometimes look to sexual relationships as a means of approval, which they lack from their father.

3. All sexual activity that is not within God's definition _____ the blessings that God intended for man and woman.

   a. Sexual sins come from the _____ of your will and it affects how your spirit relates to God, others, and yourself.

   b. Webster's Dictionary defines sex as: anything connected with sexual _____ or arousal or reproduction. By definition, French kissing is sex, foreplay is sex, oral sex is sex, masturbation is sex, etc.

> *"People conceived and brought into life by God don't make a practice of sin. How could they? God's seed is deep within them, making them who they are. It's not in the nature of the God-begotten to practice and parade sin. Here's how you tell the difference between God's children and the devil's children: The one who won't practice righteous ways isn't from God, nor is the one who won't love brother or sister. A simple test."*
>
> **I John 3:9** (The Message)

> *"There's more to sex than mere skin on skin. Sex is as much spiritual mystery as physical fact. As written in Scripture, "The two become one." Since we want to become spiritually one with the Master, we must not pursue the kind of sex that avoids commitment and intimacy, leaving us more lonely than ever—the kind of sex that can never "become one." There is a sense in which sexual sins are different from all others. In sexual sin we violate the sacredness of our own bodies, these bodies that were made for God-given and God-modeled love, for "becoming one" with another. Or didn't you realize that your body is a sacred place, the place of the Holy Spirit? Don't you see that you can't live however you please, squandering what God paid such a high price for? The physical part of you is not some piece of property belonging to the spiritual part of you. God owns the whole works. So let people see God in and through your body."*
>
> **I Corinthians 6: 16-20** (The Message)

4. Often if you commit fornication or adultery you will say you fell in love and then out of love. Fornication is sexual intimacy _____ marriage. Adultery _____ the covenant of marriage. Adultery is breaking the 7th commandment.

    The reality is that they fell into hate not love.

    Fornication and adultery includes manipulating one another for self-pleasure. When you commit sexual sin, you flaunt all that is holy for selfish reasons. Immorality is ugly and destructive.

5   An unintended consequence of sex outside of marriage is an unplanned pregnancy. The impact of an _____ is significant and can last for decades.

    Of women who have abortions, 62% have religious affiliation. Yet, very few churches talk about abortion or provide help for those who've had one. Abortion can be a silent killer of the soul, *(see pages 229-234 for post abortive healing).*

Abortion is associated with more stress and anxiety. And Post Abortive women are twice as likely to feel guilt and 60% feel shame. Men also suffer from guilt and remorse based on their involvement in an abortion, but they are often not even recognized in the conversation.

How long will you carry the guilt and grief of your painful decision? God forgave you the first time you asked for it. He says your sin is as far away as the east is from the west (Psalm 103:12). God promises to those who mourn that He will bestow on you a crown of beauty for your ashes (Isaiah 61:3).

No person who is truly a lover ever _____ another. In using others, you demolish the glory of God designed for blessings.

> *"But My people have exchanged their Glory for worthless idols."*
>
> **Jeremiah 2:11b** (NIV)

Symptoms of the Door of Sexual Sin that we open up to the enemy. Check any of these that apply to you:

- ❏ Promiscuity
- ❏ Lasciviousness
- ❏ Lewdness
- ❏ Lust
- ❏ Adultery
- ❏ Fornication
- ❏ Pornography
- ❏ Sexual Books, movies, games
- ❏ Abortion
- ❏ Gender Confusion/Transgender
- ❏ Homosexuality
- ❏ Bisexuality
- ❏ Transvestites
- ❏ Lesbianism
- ❏ Pedophilia
- ❏ Other_____
- ❏ Other_____

6. If you have committed sexual sins, it is important to look for the _____ _____ for the choice you made.

7. Besides healing the root, it is also important to break _____ _____ with your sexual partners.

    a. Any sexual act _____ a person's spirit with the spirit of another.

> *"Do you not know that he who unites himself with a prostitute is one with her in body? For it is said, 'The two will become one flesh.'"*
>
> **I Corinthians 6:16**

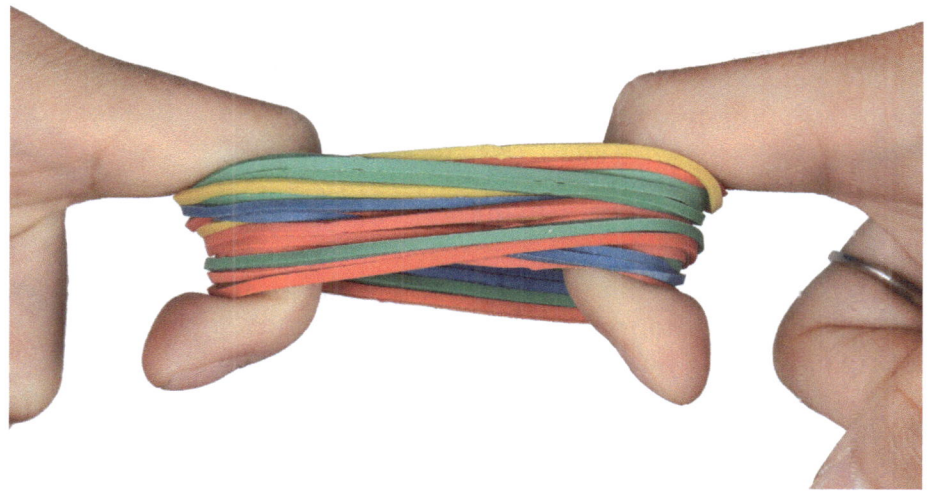

In the sexual act, you become knitted together and your spirit remembers the union. These unions can be thought of as large _____ _____.

> The rubber band is what binds you together, even after the sexual act is over. For each sexual partner there is a different rubber band. If you have many sexual partners, you will experience increasing bondage as the rubber bands tying you to your partners become tighter and tighter.

b. The first sexual union is the most important because a _____ covenant is established when the female's hymen is broken (and bleeds). The only way to break that covenant is the blood covenant of Jesus Christ.

c. If you have been _____ , the demon of rape may harass you because it was taken from you. You will need to break the soul ties with your rapist.

Rape and Incest are significant problems in the United States.

Rape: Approximately 70% of rape or sexual assault victims experience moderate to severe distress, a larger percentage than for any other violent crime. It's estimated that more than a million rape kits have never been processed. Rape is underreported and under believed leaving the victims further traumatized by the system who are supposed to protect and serve them.

Incest: One in three-to-four girls, and one in five-to-seven boys are sexually abused before they turn 18, an overwhelming incidence of which happens *within* the family. These statistics are well known among industry professionals, who are often quick to add, *and this is a notoriously <u>underreported</u> crime.*

The pervasiveness of shame, guilt, self-loathing and self-directed disgust experienced by many incest victims cannot be overstated. Victims of incest are found in all walks of life and from all socio-economic circumstances. You suffer from significant psychological trauma including disassociation.

If you've been a victim of rape or incest, please look on pages 234-235 for a healing prayer.

8. Adultery not only breaks the marriage covenant, but also brings upon yourself a curse of _____ (read Numbers 5:11-31). If you divorced your spouse because your spouse committed adultery, you need to deal with the spirit of

    _____.

    There is an incalculable cost to infidelity. Not just with the loss of trust but because the destruction created by unfaithfulness is a deep emotional wound that takes time to heal. The cheater must uncover the root cause of why you cheated while the beloved left out often suffers from anger, hurt, betrayal, grief, depression and an emptiness that can only be filled by Jesus. Both spouses lose the important connection power of physical touch, both sexual and nonsexual, they need to recover from a devastating loss.

    Once an affair is found out, fear and anxiety may actually intensify as an unintended consequence. The added difficulty of resistance to forgive makes the price of infidelity significant. Giving up the records/account of infidelity is absolutely essential. But with God, healing is possible even with infidelity (Matthew 17:20).

"The man who hates and divorces his wife," says the Lord, the God of Israel, "does violence to the one he should protect," says the Lord Almighty. So be on your guard, and do not be unfaithful."

Malachi 2:16

> *"Our Hero, come and rescue us! O God of the breakthrough, for the glory of Your name, come and help us! Forgive and restore us; heal us and cover us in Your love."*
>
> **Psalm 79:9**

9. Involvement with _____ is found in the Bible – "poreneuf" is translated as the word "adultery" in Mark 10:19a. Pornography is the "carbon monoxide poisoning" of the church because you can't see it, yet it destroys people.

> *"You know the commandments: 'Do not murder, do not commit adultery, do not steal, do not give false testimony, do not defraud, honor your father and mother.'"*
>
> **Mark 10:19**

Pornography is something you don't want to talk about but it is a real struggle for many Christians. You can't heal what you don't reveal. Pornography creates so much shame that it can be soul-crushing and it has physical consequences as well.

Unless you get to the root, the fruit of your behavior won't change. Isn't it time for you to give up your secrets, your guilt, your shame, your regret to the One who died on the cross to set you free from it all?

10. When Jesus forgives He also forgets. For I will demonstrate My mercy to them and will forgive their evil deeds, and never remember again their sins (Hebrews 8:12). According to the Bible, you can do what Jesus does (John 14:12) so you can command those painful memories to leave you and they must. This has been incredibly powerful in my life for removing porn images and other painful memories. It works. Those scenes disappeared and don't replay in my mind even if I try to remember them. What a blessing! Also read Isaiah 65:16-19. Don't let the enemy torment your soul.

 **Sample Healing Prayer**

Thank you Jesus for forgiving and forgetting my sins. I command (salute) *all remembrance of* ___(painful situation)___ *to be gone from my memory in the name and blood* (touch the holes) *of Jesus Christ. Remove all memories and shame* ___(list other negative emotions)___ *of this situation from the cellular level of my body* (shake it all off) *in Jesus' name. Thank You Jesus for healing my memories and giving me rest in my soul, body, spirit, and three brains* (touch those 3 brains). Clap!

Commanding those images to go from my memory and breaking my unhealthy soul tie to pornography was the turning point in my relationship with my beloved. Here are two more helpful tips: (1) Before you are intimate, submit your spirit, soul, and body to Holy Spirit so that you come to your marriage bed with purity and love. (2) Also read out loud the sample prayer (or create your own) provided at the end of this chapter.

11. Breaking the Power of Soul Ties:

   a. To break the bondage of oneness you must confess your sexual sins. The Bible states to be specific in our prayers. This means you need to confess your sexual partners by name (first name is fine). If you have been involved with pornography you will not need to use a name of the person but still confess your sin.

b. You need to seek forgiveness for the sexual act that you just confessed. Give your records/account of wrongdoings to Jesus. It is possible to hold an account against yourself.

c. Forgive the other person involved.

d. Forgive yourself. This means to accept Christ's forgiveness. What Christ accomplished on the cross for your sins is final as well as complete.

e. If there was a blood covenant (your first sexual experience outside of marriage), break the blood covenant made with the power of the blood covenant of Jesus Christ.[††] *(see page 190)*

f. Pray to cut any soul ties between yourself and the person that you had sex with.

g. If you have been sexually molested or raped, follow these guidelines to break the power of oneness with the offender. *(see pages 234-235)*

h. If you are bitter or jealous, you will want to break that curse as well.[*] *(see page 192)*

These prayers need to be done with each sexual relationship outside the covenant of marriage. This includes any sexual relationship you had with a future spouse. For individuals that you do not remember their name, still repent and cut those ties.

Hiding Place Activation

During the Hiding Place Activation, it's best to begin with the farthest back soul tie you made. You will likely need to go through this breaking soul tie process more than one time. For some, your first soul tie was forced upon you by incest, molestation, or rape. That was likely your most traumatic soul tie and it often impacts your sexual life going forward. That's the one you will deal with today.

Sit quietly in a comfortable position. Close your eyes the entire time in a posture of prayer. Remember there will be a lot of quiet time during this activation so just relax in His Presence.

Take several deep Yah Weh breaths, letting them out slowly. Again breathe in, breathe out.

Here are some verses related to soul ties to read out loud:

"² Stop imitating the ideals and opinions of the culture around you, but be inwardly transformed by the Holy Spirit through a total reformation of how you think. This will empower you to discern God's will as you live a beautiful life, satisfying and perfect in His eyes.
        Romans 12:2

"For God will never give you the spirit of fear, but the Holy Spirit who gives you mighty power, love, and self-control.
        2 Timothy 1:7

⁸ So keep your thoughts continually fixed on all that is authentic and real, honorable and admirable, beautiful and respectful, pure and holy, merciful and kind. And fasten your thoughts on every glorious work of God, praising Him always.
        Philippians 4:8

For the mind-set of the flesh is death, but the mind-set controlled by the Spirit finds life and peace.
        Romans 8:6

Then, you're going to pray Psalm 31: 20 over yourself:

²⁰ So hide me Your beloved one in the sheltered, secret hiding place before Your face. Overshadow me by Your glory-presence…Tuck me safely away in the tabernacle where You dwell.

Lord, I want You to take me back to our hiding place now. Go back with Him to your hiding place. Then rest in His Presence and love for as long as you like.

Praying Scripture Prior to Breaking Your Soul Tie(s):

Pray from Psalm 139:23-24. Say out loud: *"God, I invite Your searching gaze into my heart. Examine me through and through; find out everything that may be hidden within me. Put me to the test and sift through all my anxious cares. See if there is any path of pain I'm walking on, and lead me back to Your glorious, everlasting ways— the path that brings me back to You."*

Now, you're going to invite Jesus to bring you back to your soul tie situation by asking Jesus: *Jesus, show me the earliest situation where I made a soul tie. I trust You to keep me safe and secure in Your love.* Write down what you see/hear/feel/know.

Say: *Jesus, show me where You were in this situation.* Write down what you see/hear/feel/know.

_____

_____

_____

Say: *Jesus show me what lie(s) I believed in that situation.* Write down what you see/hear/feel/know.

_____

_____

_____

Say: *Jesus, what is Your Truth about me from this situation?* Write down what you see/hear/feel/know.

_____

_____

_____

Now ask Him: *Jesus, please show me the pain that this soul tie has cost me in my life.* Write down what you hear/see/sense.

_____

_____

_____

Jesus, what records/account of wrongdoing have I been holding on to that I need to give to You?

_____

_____

_____

Ask Jesus: *Jesus, show me if I am suffering from any physical or emotional dis-ease due to my soul tie? Please tell me because I want to be healed.* Write down what you hear/see/sense.

_____

_____

_____

Now ask Him: *Jesus, in what ways has this soul tie negatively affected my life?* Write down what you hear/see/sense.

_____

_____

_____

If your first sexual experience was incest, molestation, or rape we need to break the soul tie with the rapist and command the demon of rape to leave you because your purity was taken from you.

++ To break a blood covenant in your first intercourse experience, SAY: *In the name of Jesus Christ and by the power of His blood* (touch the holes), *I break the blood covenant with* _____(name)_____ . *This covenant no longer has a hold on me. I command* (point where it should go) *the demon of rape to leave me* (slash). *You have no right* (shake head no) *to harass me because Jesus died on the cross to save me and He has made me pure, blameless and spotless, in the powerful name of Jesus.* Clap!

Sample Healing Prayer to Break Unhealthy Sexual Soul Ties

In the name of Jesus Christ and the power of His blood (touch the holes), *I break* (slash) *the power of all ungodly spirit, soul and bodily* (touch each one) *ties between* _____(name)_____ *and me. By the power of the cross* (cross sign), *I send back to* _____(name)_____ *all parts of him/her* (take them out of your soul) *that s/he gave to me that never belonged to me washed in the blood of Jesus for purity's sake. And I take back from* _____(name)_____ *all parts of me* (bring them back to you) *that I gave to him/her that never belonged to him/her washed in the blood of Jesus for purity's sake.*

Please forgive me (bow down to Him)*Jesus for my unhealthy soul tie. I accept Your forgiveness of my sin and Your complete restoration. I forgive* _____(name)_____ *for their involvement. I give to You* (hand them over) *Jesus, all my records/account of wrongdoing. What do You want to do with these records Jesus?*_____

_____

I choose by an act of my will to forgive myself for my part and I break off (slash) *any shame and pain* (shake it off) *from my soul* (touch your head) *connected to this unhealthy soul tie in Jesus name.*

In Jesus Christ's name, I command (salute) *complete healing and restoration of* _____(disease)_____ *caused by my soul tie(s). By Your stripes* (touch the holes) *I am healed. Thank you Jesus.*

Father, I ask you to set a guard (place a guard over your head, heart and body) *over my spirit, soul and body to never again connect with* _____(name)_____ *in any ungodly way. I sever* (cut them) *the ties from my soul, spirit, and body* (touch all 3). *I am free* (wave hands) *and* _____(name)_____ *is set free. I nail* (use hammer) *to the cross the lie that joining with* _____(name)_____ *in these ungodly ways was necessary, needed, or wanted on my part. I break* (slash) *all agreements I've made with this soul tie known or unknown and I turn away* (turn around) *from joining with it.*

I commit (clasp hands) *this day to walk out my healing and commitment with Jesus' help by His blood* (touch crucifixion nail holes) *and in His* (point up) *powerful name:* Clap!

_____<signature>_____<date>_____.

Jump up into the victory stance and shout *"I have victory in Jesus!"*

Jesus, what will You give me in exchange for my records/account of wrongdoing in my soul tie?

_____

_____

i.†† To break a blood covenant, add: *In the name of Jesus Christ and by the power of His blood, I break the blood covenant with _____(name)_____. This covenant no longer has a hold upon me.*

j.* If bitterness or jealousy was involved, add: *In Jesus Christ's name and by the power of His blood* (touch the holes), *I break* (sever it) *the curse of bitterness (or jealousy) that has entered me because of the adulteress relationship with _____(name)_____ . This curse no longer* (shake head no) *has a hold upon me. I am forgiven.* Clap!

Sample Healing Prayer for Unhealthy Non-Sexual Soul Ties

Both prayers dapted from: Erin Lamb https://ithoughtiknewwhatlovewas.com

In Jesus name, I break (cut it) *any connection of mine to _(name)_____ in the soul/spirit realm that's not of God. I command any parts of their soul attached to mine to be released back to them* (take them out of your soul) *cleansed in the blood of Jesus* (touch the holes) *and free of any demonic spirits.*

I command any spirits not of the Holy Spirit that attached to me or came to me through this bond to leave (pull them out and send them to Jesus) *and go to Jesus never to return to me. I choose by an act of my will to forgive _____(name)_____ and me for my part and I break off any shame and pain* (shake it off) *from my soul connected to this unhealthy soul tie in Jesus name.*

I ask God for a wall of fire (welcome the fire around you) *around my soul, spirit and body so nothing from them not of You passes into me. I call back any parts of my soul linked to them, cleansed in the blood of Jesus* (touch the holes) *and free of any demonic spirits. They are free, and I am free in Jesus name.* Clap! Jump up into the victory stance and shout "victory in Jesus"!

Healing Your Soul

Sample Prayer to Use Before Intimacy with a Spouse Who Has Not Yet Done Soul Healing (this protects you from receiving anything not of God from him/her)

 *God, thank You for my union with my beloved. I thank You for them and our intimacy. I want all the good that flows through my beloved* (point to them) *to flow into me* (point to self). *I do not want anything that is not of You to have access to me. I bind* (squeeze hands) *any spirits that are not of Your spirit from entering me through our soul tie and covenant.*

I am not in agreement with any of my beloved's sin. I break (slash) *agreement with any of my beloved's sin and command* (salute) *any spirits we share in common to go to a dry uninhabited place* (send them to the pit). *I ask God for a wall of fire* (welcome the fire around you) *around my soul, spirit, and body so nothing from them not of You passes into me.*

In the name of Jesus, I break (slash) *any ungodly portions of my soul tie* (touch head) *with my beloved and command* (salute) *any spirits from my beloved* (point to them) *to go to a dry uninhabited place* (pull them out and send them to Jesus), *never to return. My soul* (touch head) *is a no access area* (shake your head no) *to demons. When we are physically or emotionally intimate, I forbid* (cross your arms) *any spirits from entering my body or soul* (touch body and head).

I ask for purifying fire (welcome the fire) *on our union. I pray* (prayer clasp) *for the soul healing and restoration of my beloved* (point to them). *Lord may my healing be a catalyst for my beloved's freedom. In Jesus' powerful name, Amen.* Clap!

Breakthrough Decrees (repeat daily)
(activate your words with body action)

1. I am sexually pure and honor God with my body (I Corinthians 6:18-20; I Thessalonians 4:3-7; Hebrews 13:4).

2. God's love and peace is in my relationships (Colossians 3:14).

3. I exercise self-control and show love to others without creating unhealthy soul ties (1 Corinthians 13:4-5).

4. I prosper in my relationships (Luke 2:52).

5. I consistently bring God encounters to others (Mark 16:17,18).

6. My truth to replace the lie: _____.

On this day _____, I establish these decrees that are founded in God's Word.

Signed: _____

 **Resources**

Moral Revolution: The Naked Truth About Sexual Purity, Kris Vallotton, Chosen Books, 2012.

Rape Statistics:
https://www.rainn.org/statistics/victims-sexual-violence

Incest Research:
https://www.psychiatrictimes.com/view/ramifications-incest

Homework This Week

1. Make a list of sexual partners or sex acts that you need to pray through. Ask the Holy Spirit to reveal any other soul ties that you have made. Ask Holy Spirit to show you any root causes that you need to deal with that caused you to make unhealthy soul ties.

_____

_____

_____

_____

_____

_____

_____

2. Say out loud this week's Breakthrough Decrees daily.

3. Write in your Victory and Gratitude Journals.

4. Continue participating in the weekly Mentoring Moment.

Your Victory Journal

_____

_____

_____

_____

_____

_____

_____

_____

_____

_____

_____

_____

_____

_____

_____

_____

_____

_____

_____

_____

_____

_____

_____

_____

_____

_____

_____

_____

_____

Daily Gratitude Journal

Write down 3 things you are thankful or grateful for each day.

Date:_____1. _____

2. _____

3. _____

Date:_____1. _____

2. _____

3. _____

Date:_____1. _____

2. _____

3. _____

Date:_____1. _____

2. _____

3. _____

Date:_____1. _____

2. _____

3. _____

Date:_____1. _____

2. _____

3. _____

Date:_____1. _____

2. _____

3. _____

Date:_____1. _____

2. _____

3. _____

Date:_____1. _____

2. _____

3. _____

Fill-in-the-Blank Answer Guide

1. male
   female
   oneness
2. love
   a. protect
   b. nurture
   c. disrespect
3. distorts
   a. choices
   b. gratification
4. before
   violates
5. abortion   uses
6. root cause
7. soul ties
   a. unites
      rubber bands
   b. blood
   c. raped
8. bitterness
   jealousy
9. pornography

Walking In Victory

T he biggest question you may have now is, "How do I walk this out?" The greatest answer is partner with THEM in everything you do. Let's talk practically about how to do that.

1. The Heart _____ is the sum of who you are. The condition of your heart determines the quality of your character. How do you respond when pressure hits you? When your response isn't what you want, ask yourself, "Why did I respond that way?" Holy Trinity will guide you through your healing by going back to the root and do the Divine Exchange as you've learned in each lesson.

Your Heart and how you think, speak and what you do must be done with THEM in partnership with you. The 30 Second Rule is huge! You cannot hold on to thinking that becomes toxic to you and those around you. With THEM, you are a demon slayer.

> *"You have minds like a snake pit! How do you suppose what you say is worth anything when you are so foul-minded? It's your heart, not the dictionary, that gives meaning to your words. A good person produces good deeds and words season after season. An evil person is a blight on the orchard. Let me tell you something: Every one of these careless words is going to come back to haunt you. There will be a time of Reckoning. Words are powerful; take them seriously. Words can be your salvation. Words can also be your damnation."*
>
> **Matthew 12:34-37** (The Message)

2. The key to victory is being _____ into THEM. Jesus is the vine and you are His branch. You are integrated into THEM and THEY are integrated into you. This means you are intentionally aware of partnering with THEM in all you think, say and do. The sap that flows through THEM also flows through you as a branch.

> *"I am a true sprouting vine, and the farmer who tends the vine is My Father. He cares for the branches connected to Me by lifting and propping up the fruitless branches and pruning every fruitful branch to yield a greater harvest. The words I have spoken over you have already cleansed you. So you must remain in life-union with Me, for I remain in life-union with you. For as a branch severed from the vine will not bear fruit, so your life will be fruitless unless you live your life intimately joined to Mine. I am the sprouting vine and you're My branches. As you live*

in union with Me as your source, fruitfulness will stream from within you—but when you live separated from Me you are powerless.
If a person is separated from Me, he is discarded; such branches are gathered up and thrown into the fire to be burned. But if you live in life-union with Me and if My words live powerfully within you—then you can ask whatever you desire and it will be done."

John 15:1-7

Naturally, it is easier to produce the fruit of the spirit without effort simply by "being" in THEM. Then that fruit flows out to others as well.

"When your lives bear abundant fruit, you demonstrate that you are My mature disciples who glorify My Father! I love each of you with the same love that the Father loves Me. You must continually let My love nourish your hearts. If you keep My commands, you will live in My love, just as I have kept My Father's commands, for I continually live nourished and empowered by His love."

John 15: 8-10

3. The _____ of your heart is a real place where you may put people when you want to remember what they did to you so you are protected. You may forgive with your mouth but you need THEM to help you forgive from your body, soul and spirit that hold your memories, as well as your three brains (gut, head, heart). While you did healing work on the three brains in lesson 2, if you are still struggling with self-protection then here's another healing prayer for you:

Healing Prayer

Father God, everything _____(person's name aho hurt you)_____ *did to me was on You Jesus when You were on the cross. Jesus bought all your sins, just like HE bought mine. By a choice of my free will, I choose to forgive* _____(name)_____ *for*_____(actiuon against me)_____ *. I give you my feel-ings* _____(emotions)_____ *as I no longer want to carry those in my soul or body* (touch your head and body).

Jesus, unlock the prison of my heart (put your hand over your heart) *and escort* _____(name)_____ *out* (show them the way) *out. I choose to forgive you* _____(name)_____ *and I turn you over* (hand them over) *to You Jesus to become the man/woman, You created them to be. Bye Bye*_____(name)_____ *please go to Jesus with my blessings.*

Jesus, I give to You any and all records of wrongs (give them to Jesus) *that I have held against* _____(name)_____. *Show me what You want to do with those records.* Please write what you see along with the date.

_____

_____ date _____

Jesus, please take me into Your arms and remove all the poison, fiery darts, arrows, daggers and pins (take them out) *that were inserted into me by the enemy through* _____(name and situation)_____.
Take all the works of the enemy in my mind, will, and emotions (touch your head), *which is my soul, my body and my spirit all away. Heal my head, gut and heart brains* (touch each brain) *from the works of the enemy. Absorb it completely and let me feel all of that trauma and drama leave me now.* Take a moment to feel it all leave you.

Holy Spirit, divinely edit out (writing motion) *whatever is causing me pain, rejection, abandonment, shame, guilt, physical problems, lies, inner vows, any list of wrongs, in the name of Jesus and by His blood* (touch the holes).

Holy Spirit I ask You to divinely edit (writing motion) *out any and all memories from my mind* (touch head) *regarding any events that hap-pened and to remove* (push away) *the memory of all the wrong touches*

Healing Your Soul

from my skin and my body, removing (push away) *all the trauma in Jesus Name and by His blood* (touch the holes).

Holy Spirit, what will You give me (hands out) *in exchange for all this trauma/drama* _____

_____

I receive (hands out) *Your divine exchange in Jesus name. I pray this in Your name and by Your blood* (touch the holes) *that bought this for me. Amen.*

Write out a decree of Truth to counter the lie(s) you've believed as a result of your prayer:

_____

Please add this Truth to your list of Breakthrough Decrees at the end of this lesson.

I commit this day to walk out my healing with Jesus' help by His blood and in His powerful name*: Clap!+

_____ <signature> _____ <date> _____ .

4. Three Steps to Walk in _____
   Step 1: Partner with the HOLY TRINITY in everything you do. Examples: Take your shower or bath with THEM, Brush your teeth with THEM, shave with THEM, talk to THEM about your life out loud.
   Step 2. Live in the now with THEM. You can't have a do over from yesterday. Tomorrow is always in the future but now is where THEY are. Spell NOW backwards = WON. Together with THEM you will have WON every battle!
   Step 3: Commit to a love walk with THEM. THEY will help you navigate life.

A Re-Evaluation of Scale of Your Closeness of Your Relationship with THEM

With this in mind-the scale starts as 0 being the greatest distance from you that you feel THEY can be and 10 being the closest to you.

PANE Scale	Far Distance										Closest
Distance from Father God	0	1	2	3	4	5	6	7	8	9	10
Distance from Jesus Christ	0	1	2	3	4	5	6	7	8	9	10
Distance from Holy Spirit	0	1	2	3	4	5	6	7	8	9	10

How have these numbers changed for you over this course?

_____

_____

With this same scale let's look at your Identity with the 0 meaning you know nothing about your identity in Father God, Jesus and Holy Spirit and who you are in THEM. A 5 meaning you know somewhat and a 10 meaning you know exactly who you are in THEM.

	Know Nothing								I Know Who I Am		
Identity Scale	0	1	2	3	4	5	6	7	8	9	10

How has this number changed?

_____

_____

With this same scale let's look at how heavy you feel as to the burden you carry? O means you feel none at all, 5 feels somewhat of a burden and a 10 meaning it can't get any heavier. Please circle one.

	No Burden			Somewhat				Heaviest Burden		
Burden Scale	0	1	2	3	4	5	6	7	8	9	10

Where are you now with carrying your burdens?

_____

_____

5. Your greatest challenge in walking in victory may be your intent and _____ .

Let's divide the scripture John 10:10 into two parts.
  1) The intent of the enemy, satan, the hater of my soul. "*The thief comes to kill steal and destroy*"
  2) The intent of Jesus, the lover of my soul. "*but I came that you may have life and have it more abundantly.*"

This scripture holds the intent (goals) of the kingdom of darkness (satan) in contrast to the intent (goal) of the Kingdom of Light which is THEM. The decision is yours to make - which intent will you choose? God's or satan's?

Agreement, is the decision you act upon. Each day and every moment you will come into agreement with one of those intents.

You are designed by God to think good thoughts. 2 Corinthians 10:5 "*We can demolish **every** deceptive fantasy that opposes God and break through every arrogant attitude that is raised up in defiance of the true knowledge of God. We capture, like prisoners of war, every thought and insist that it bow in obedience to the Anointed One.*"

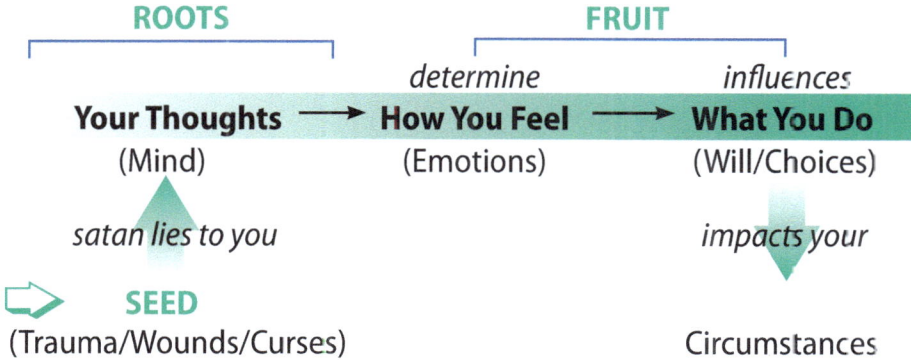

You are not designed for bad thoughts but this is what satan wants for you. Your mental health is determined by your thinking. Your actions are determined by what you think about. What you focus on is what you make room for in your life. Your thoughts determine who you become.

You are designed by God for love.

> *"The one who doesn't love has yet to know God, for God is love."*
>
> **1 John 4:8**
>
> *"For God will never give you the spirit of fear, but the Holy Spirit who gives you mighty power, love, and self-control."*
>
> **2 Timothy 1:7**

Fear is a learned thinking pattern that is inspired and authored by satan in your life. Fear wants to sit as king of your mind, body, and heart. Jesus is the author and finisher of your Faith.

> *"Looking unto Jesus the author and finisher of our faith; who for the joy that was set before Him endured the cross, despising the shame, and is set down at the right hand of the throne of God."*
>
> **Hebrews 12:2**

The intent of your enemy satan is to establish these problems in your life:
1. Rule from a throne of fear in your mind.
2. Ruin the purpose God created you for.
3. Take away your passion for the purpose God implanted in you (Jeremiah 29:11).
4. Take away your hope and future.
5. Rob you of the dreams that God has put in you.
6. Remove the talents and gifts that God has blessed you with.
7. Remove any potential greatness that God has planned for you through the destiny that God chose for your life to give you pleasure.

In fact you were made for His pleasure. He takes joy in seeing the happiness He can bring to you as His companion, allowing you to fulfill the purpose for which He created you.

> *"For the LORD delights in His people; He crowns the humble with victory."*
>
> **Psalm 149:4**

You are designed by God in His image.

> *"So God created human beings in His own image. In the image of God He created them; male and female He created them."*
>
> **Genesis 1:27**

When God wove you in your mother's womb, you only knew His love and kindness. You did not have fear until you experienced trauma in the womb (lesson 3) and/or mankind instilled that input into your mind. Science has proven that humankind is not born with structures of fear [1], God created you with only structures of love in your brain. The enemy has given you lies of fear because he is only knows hate. That's what he wants for you.

What is your decision (i.e. agreement)? Do you want to change your agreement or do you allow satan to continue stealing, killing and destroying your life? Understand that in every life event there is an intent of the enemy. Now that you see that intent, it's easier to forgive the humans involved in the event so you can let go of your bondage and captivity that un-forgiveness brings.

 **Personal Application/Exercise**

Personal Application: The question to ask in any difficult situation is, Holy Trinity what was the enemy's intent through
_____(person)_____ against me? Wait for the answer. If there is none then ask: Holy Trinity what does the enemy want to steal, kill, or destroy in my life?_____.

Once you are aware of the enemy's intent, do not come into agreement with him but instead let the sacrifice of Jesus do all it was meant to do. Jesus takes your sin as His curse on the cross. Then do the Divine Exchange. Now it becomes easier to see how the enemy is trying to victimize you through another's actions. Let go of the event, the pain it caused, and forgive the other person and set them free. Now you are free!

6. The _____ door of your heart is a new way of looking at Revelation 3:20

"Behold, I'm standing at the door, knocking. If your heart is open to hear My voice and you open the door within, I will come in to you and feast with you, and you will feast with Me."

Revelation 3:20

We typically read this verse for salvation but this verse speaks about Holy Trinity wanting to fellowship with you! When you have walls up, this love door cannot be fully open to THEM. But, when this love door is fully open to THEM, all the doors of the enemy remain shut.

That means the doors of anger, hatred, fear, sexual sin and the occult (which we covered in other lessons) will not be open and cannot open, when your love door to THEM is fully open!

> *"People are known in this same way. Out of the virtue stored in their hearts, good and upright people will produce good fruit. Likewise, out of the evil hidden in their hearts, evil ones will produce what is evil. For the overflow of what has been stored in your heart will be seen by your fruit and will be heard in your words."*
>
> **Luke 6:45**

> *"God, who knows the hearts of every person, confirmed this when He gave them the Holy Spirit, just like He has given the Spirit to us."*
>
> **Acts 15:8**

The greatest commandment is that we love each other as much as THEY love us and that we demonstrate His love to others.

> *"So I give you now a new commandment: Love each other just as much as I have loved you. For when you demonstrate the same love I have for you by loving one another, everyone will know that you're My true followers."*
>
> **John 13:34-35**

While love is a commandment, it's not the only reason loving others makes you feel better. Research shows that depression, anxiety, and stress often center around self-focused thoughts. When you help others it can actually transform your mindset and replace negative emotions.[2]

Let's demonstrate Jesus' love by helping others. Together we can find ways to heal our world and make it a better place to live.

7. Change your _____!

You've done the hard work. You've experienced many break-throughs. You've told those negative memories and emotions to leave. The day you start taking responsibility for yourself, is the day you grow up.

Now it's time to go and activate your future. You've been given the tools in this book and course to heal your past. You can come back to this tool chest any time you need more healing. Soul healing often comes in layers. Read your decrees daily. Write new daily decrees to read and get them deep into your body, soul and spirit.

Focus on where you want to go, not on what you fear. You can't live life looking in the rearview mirror because it doesn't allow you to see your future. The future THEY want for you. The future you want for you. So rise up and change your story. Welcome to your healed life!

Personal Note from the Authors:

We want to encourage you on the great job you have done in being faithful to complete your soul healing journey, this far. We also want to remind you that every tear you have cried, THEY stored each one of them, because those tears are precious to THEM. THEY care that much about you. Tears and healing your soul is THEIR greatest priority.

THEY do not have a to-do-list, as Patti says, THEY want your love. THEY want you to just love THEM and allow THEM to dwell in you so THEY can help you live life. THEY want the real, true you to know the real, true THEM. That is THEIR only goal with you. Soul healing is the biggest investment you will ever make, in yourself. That is what is important to THEM, that you learn to just "be" in THEM and then allow THEM to just "be' in you.

This chapter is the summation of all you have learned so far, plus a little bit more. It covers a lot of critical areas because it is the end chapter before you are launched as the new you in THEM. You will from now on be that new you in THEM and THEY in you. We call it coming into ONENESS with THEM. John chapter 17 is where you will find this information.

We pray our book will fine tune you into what THEY want for you. When you use these tools like we do, you will revisit this book often, because life happens. Learn these tools and employ them in your life, they will soon become your auto pilot of peace and joy.

We Bless You and Pray for You in Jesus name, Keren and Patti

Breakthrough Decrees (repeat daily)
(activate your words with body action)

1. I am engrafted in THEM and moment by moment I partner with THEM (John 15:1-7). I am a new creation in Christ (2Corinthians 5:17).

2. I walk in victory and agreement with Jesus so fear has no place in me (2 Corinthians 10:5) and I destroy the works of the devil (Hebrews 2:14).

3. I love and serve others well and my breakthroughs encourage others (John 13: 34-35).

4. God has given me a new story and I walk in victory! (Colossians 1:21-22; Titus 3:5)

5. My truth to replace the lie:_____.

    On this day _____, I establish these decrees that are founded in God's Word.

    Signed: _____

Homework This Week

Look through all the decrees you've made in this course (pages 23, 46, 68, 100, 123, 151, 172, 194, 214) and select the decrees you want to make daily to begin your new story. Continually come back to these pages and/or make your own decrees with Scripture as a regular habit in your life.

_____

_____

_____

_____

_____

_____

_____

_____

_____

_____

_____

_____

_____

_____

_____

_____

_____

_____

_____

_____

_____

_____

_____

_____

_____

_____

_____

_____

_____

Victory Journal of Your Progress

_____   _____
_____   _____
_____   _____
_____   _____
_____   _____
_____   _____
_____   _____

Use additional pages if you need more room.

Daily Gratitude Journal

Write down 3 things you are thankful or grateful for each day.

Date:_____1. _____
2. _____
3. _____
Date:_____1. _____
2. _____
3. _____
Date:_____1. _____
2. _____
3. _____
Date:_____1. _____
2. _____
3. _____
Date:_____1. _____
2. _____
3. _____

Fill-in-the-Blank Answer Guide

1. condition
2. engrafted
3. prison
4. victory
5. agreement
6. love
7. story

Resources

(1) The Biology of Fear. National Library of Medicine, Ralph Adolphs. January 21, 2013.
https://www.ncbi.nlm.nih.gov/pmc/articles/PMC3595162/

(2) New Research Shows that Helping Others May be the Key. Lisa Farino. G.O. Community Development Corporation, April 25, 2017. https://www.go-cdc.org/2017/new-research-shows-that-helping-others-may-be-the-key-to-happiness/ to happiness.

Bonus Materials

How Can I Be Saved?

> *"And this is the testimony: God has given us eternal life, and this life is in His Son. He who has the Son has life; he who does not have the Son of God does not have life."*
>
> **1 John 5:11-12 (NIV)**

This passage tells us that God has given us eternal life and this life is in His Son, Jesus Christ. In other words, the way to possess eternal life is to possess God's Son. The question is how can a person have the Son of God?

Man's Problem

Separation From God

On one side of the bridge is God. On the other side are people. Between God and people is a great gap, a division that exists because of our tendency to rebel against God's way and go our own way instead. This is what the Bible calls "sin."

> *"But your iniquities have made a separation between you and God, And your sins have hidden His face from you, so that He does not hear."*
>
> **Isaiah 59:2** (English Standard Version)

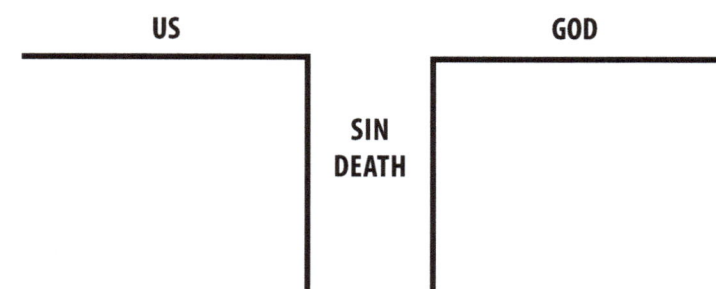

The Uselessness of Our Works

The dilemma that we face is that we want to get to God, but we know we can't just leap over the gap. So we try using human effort to build a bridge until we finally realize that all the human effort in the world will never be enough to get us to the other side.

The Bible teaches that no amount of human goodness, works, morality, or religious activity can gain acceptance with God or get anyone into heaven. We all fall short of God's perfect righteousness.

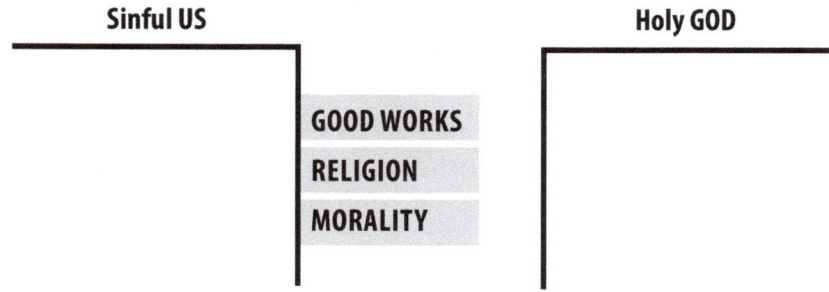

After discussing the immoral man, the moral man, and the religious man in Romans 1:18-3:8, the Apostle Paul declares that both Jews and Greeks are under sin, that "there is none righteous, not even one" (Rom. 3:9-10). Added to this are the following verses from the Bible:

> *"For it is by grace you have been saved, through faith—and this not from yourselves, it is the gift of God—not by works, so that no one can boast."*
>
> **Ephesians 2:3-9 (NIV)**

> *"He saved us, not because of righteous things we had done, but because of His mercy. He saved us through the washing of rebirth and renewal by the Holy Spirit, whom He poured out on us generously through Jesus Christ our Savior, so that, having been justified by His grace, we might become heirs having the hope of eternal life."*
>
> **Titus 3:5-7 (NIV)**

He takes us as we are and works with us. When we turn to THEM for salvation we receive the righteousness of Jesus Christ. We will never get to the place where we don't need to grow more in THEM.

God's Solution

Thankfully, God sympathized with our dilemma and because He loves us so much, He intervened so that we can have a way to getting close to Him. His solution was to choose His only Son Jesus Christ to serve as a bridge.

> *"But God demonstrates His own love toward us in this: while we were still sinners, Christ died for us."*
>
> **Romans 5:8 (NIV)**

According to Romans 5:8, God demonstrated His love for us through the death of His Son. Why did Christ have to die for us? Because Scripture declares all men to be sinful. To "sin" means to miss the mark. The Bible declares "all have sinned and fall short of the glory (the perfect holiness) of God" (Rom. 3:23). In other words, our sin separates us from God who is perfect holiness (righteousness and justice) and God must therefore judge sinful man.

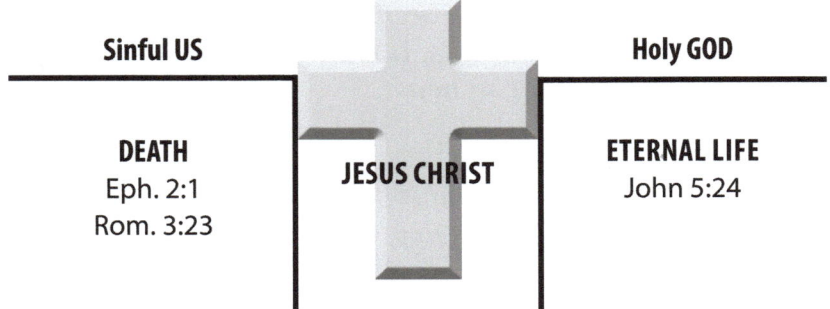

Sinful US		Holy GOD
DEATH	**JESUS CHRIST**	**ETERNAL LIFE**
Eph. 2:1		John 5:24
Rom. 3:23		

This is the message of the gospel. It's the message of the gift of God's own Son who became man (the God-man), lived a sinless life, died on the cross to become payment for our sin and was raised from the grave proving both the fact He is God's Son and the value of His death for us as our substitute. Jesus became our *bridge* to God and Eternal Life.

> *"I tell you the truth, whoever hears My word and believes Him who sent Me has eternal life and will not be condemned; he has crossed over from death to life."*
>
> **John 5:24** (NIV)
>
> *"He was delivered over to death for our sins and was raised to life for our justification."*
>
> **Romans 4:25** (NIV)
>
> *"God made Him who had no sin to be sin for us, so that in Him we might become the righteousness of God."*
>
> **2 Corinthians 5:21** (NIV)

How Do We Receive God's Son?

Because of what Jesus Christ accomplished for us on the cross, the Bible states "He that has the Son has life." We can receive the Son, Jesus Christ, as our Savior by trusting in the person of Christ and His death for our sins.

> *"Yet to all who received Him, to those who believed in His name, He gave the right to become children of God—"*
>
> **John 1:12 (N V)**
>
> *"For God so loved the world that He gave His one and only Son, that whoever believes in Him shall not perish but have eternal life. For God did not send His Son into the world to condemn the world, but to save the world through Him. Whoever believes in Him is not condemned, but whoever does not believe stands condemned already because he has not believed in the name of God's one and only Son."*
>
> **John 3:16-18 (NIV)**

This means we must each come to God the same way:
1. as a sinner who recognizes his/her sinfulness,
2. realizes no human works can result in salvation, and
3. relies totally on Christ alone, by faith, for our salvation.

If you would like to receive and trust Christ as your personal Savior, you may want to express your faith in Christ by a simple prayer acknowledging your sinfulness, accepting His forgiveness and putting your faith in Christ for your salvation.

Sample Prayer

"Dear Lord Jesus, I acknowledge that I am a sinner in need of Your forgiveness. I believe that You died on the cross for my sins. I repent of all my sins and I ask for Your forgiveness. Please wipe all my sins away with Your precious blood. Thank You for dying on the cross and rising from the dead to buy this freedom for me. I invite You into my heart and life and three brains and I choose to follow You as my Lord and Savior. Thank You for saving me. In Jesus' name, I pray. Amen."

Congratulations! You are a new Christ follower. This course shows you how to walk in freedom so that's a big step forward for you. THEY want nothing more than the best for you. THEY will never leave you or forsake you.

Adapted from Biblical Studies Press; www.bible.org

"Be strong and courageous, do not be afraid or tremble in dread before them, for it is the LORD your God who goes with you. He will not fail you or abandon you."

Deuteronomy 31:6 (AMP)

Where Does the Holy Spirit Fit In?

Without the Holy Spirit there is a struggle between your soul and body. Your spirit is dead. Without the Holy Spirit your soul/flesh is in control. Before you come to Christ you live from your soul and body. Your spirit is mostly inactive. The Holy Spirit gives you the power and ability to follow God.

> *"Let me emphasize this: As you yield to the dynamic life and power of the Holy Spirit, you will abandon the cravings of your self-life."*
>
> **Galatians 5:16**

a. Jesus was filled/ baptized in the Holy Spirit (John 1:32-33) just as you can be filled and empowered by the Holy Spirit.

b. Why be empowered by the Holy Spirit?

✔ He will guide you into all Truth. (John 16:13).

> *"But when the truth-giving Spirit comes, He will unveil the reality of every truth within you. He won't speak on His own, but only what He hears from the Father, and He will reveal prophetically to you what is to come."*
>
> **John 16:13**

✔ The Holy Spirit will continue to teach you all things and bring to your remembrance all that God has said through His Word (John 14:26).

> *"But when the Father sends the Spirit of Holiness, the One like Me who sets you free, He will teach you all things in My name. And He will inspire you to remember every word that I've told you."*
>
> **John 14:26**

✔ He will tell whatever He hears from the Father and He will announce to you things that are to come (John 16:13; Examples: Noah in Genesis 6:13-17; Moses in Exodus 7).

✔ He will give you a supernatural prayer language that will speak directly to God (I Corinthians 14:2)

> *"When someone speaks in tongues, no one understands a word he says, because he's not speaking to people, but to God—he is speaking intimate mysteries in the Spirit."*
>
> **1 Corinthians 14:2**

The Holy Spirit's roles:
- Convict you of sin (John 16:7-11)
- Guide and Teacher of Truth (John 16:13)
- Counselor and Helper (John 14:16)
- Fruit Producer (Galatians 5:22-23)

c. How do you become filled with the Holy Spirit? Ask! Luke 11:13

> *"If imperfect parents know how to lovingly take care of their children and give them what they need, how much more will the perfect heavenly Father give the Holy Spirit's fullness when His children ask Him."*
>
> **Luke 11:13**

Prayer: *God help me keep my spirit pure and untangled by my flesh and soul. I want to be led by Your Spirit and I ask that You daily fill my spirit with Your Holy Spirit. In Jesus Name. Amen.*

> *"The fountain of Your pleasure is found in the sacrifice of my shattered heart before You. You will not despise my tenderness as I bow down humbly at Your feet."*
>
> **Psalm 51:17**

Hiding Place Connections

IF you have problems connecting with God in your Hiding Place:

If you can't see Jesus in your hiding place, you can pray, *"Jesus, open my ears, my eyes and my heart to You. Please help me to be aware of Your presence with me here."*

Or, simply pray: *"Jesus, I need Your help. Show me what is getting in the way of me connecting to You. What do I need to do to take the next step forward"* Perhaps playing some worship music that you love may help.

Focus on Jesus and interact with Him. This may be verbal or non-verbal. You can pray, *"Lord, what do You want me to know about You? Jesus, do you have more for me in this situation? Help me to receive everything You have for me here."*

If you've not yet had an experience of connecting with God in your hiding place, some find it helpful to use positive memories and appreciation for establishing an interactive connection with God. The goal is to find a moment where you felt God's presence. Here are some examples of positive memories:

- Holding one of your children as a newborn baby
- Some other particularly beautiful experience with one of your children
- A favorite family Christmas memory
- Playing with a favorite pet
- An especially positive time with friends
- Some beautiful nature experience
- Connecting with Jesus in the context of a particularly beautiful worship service.

And then observe and describe whatever comes into your awareness.

Ask Jesus, "How do You feel about being with me?" and then observe and describe whatever comes into your awareness.

Another approach is to think of a place where you love to spend time. Invite Jesus to that place. That can be a special Hiding Place for your time with Jesus.

The purpose of spending more time in His presence builds the capacity for you to face your pain and/or trauma and give it to Jesus. This process will happen in every lesson of this transformational journey.

This was created and adapted from several resources including:
Introduction to Heart Sync Model of Healing https://ihouseofhope.com/uploads/3/4/7/5/34755627/what_is_heartsync.pdf

Strong Winds & Crashing Waves by Terry Wardle (pp. 83-85)
A Spirit-led exercise to practice the presence of the Lord https://thecounseling-moment.wordpress.com/2011/01/18/the-safe-place/
Scripture was primarily taken from The Passion Translation

Post Abortive Healing

Please know that many post abortive women (and some men) go through a more in-depth Post Abortion program or Bible Study as healing from an abortion is a journey. I've listed recommended resources from a friend who has been on this journey. She strongly recommends that someone go through these programs either in a one on one setting with a leader or in a group setting with leaders and other post abortive women (or men for a men's group).

Bible Study Curriculum Titles:
Forgiven & Set Free by Linda Cochrane
Surrendering the Secret by Pat Payton
Living in Color by Jenny McDermid

Weekend Retreats:
Deeper Still – www.GoDeeperStill.org
Rachel's Vineyard – www.RachelsVineyard.org

Healing Prayer for Those Who have had an Abortion
"Lord my God, I cried to You for help, and You healed me." (Psalm 30:2)

 **Sample Prayer**

Repeat after Me: *Oh Lord, I had an abortion and the grief and guilt I have felt ever since I made that decision has haunted me. I feel so ashamed of myself and riddled with guilt, by allowing a little life to be taken in this way.*

My heart is so heavy and I find that I am not able to think about anything else I realize more and more that it is against You Lord, that I have sinned and done this great wrong.

Lord, I feel broken inside and pray for *Your healing and comfort. You have promised to mend the broken-hearted and to set those that are captive to guilt and shame free, and Lord, You have promised forgiveness and restoration to all who come humbly to Your throne of grace and confess their wrongdoing. My hope is in You, for You alone can restore the joy of my salvation.*

Thank You, that You are a forgiving God, Your mercies are new every morning /and You have promised to carry all our guilt and burdens, and so I hand this over to You today. I ask for the healing and restoration that only You can give, and the grace to forget what is past and move on with You as my guide. I ask this all in Jesus' name, Amen.
Source: https://prayer.knowing-jesus.com/Prayer-for-Abortion

 **Sample Prayer**

Post Abortive Healing Process and Prayer for Women
"Lord my God, I cried to You for help, and You healed me." (Psalm 30:2)

Begin by praying, *"Jesus, I don't want to be chained any longer by memories of my abortion. Please come and heal me."* Now ask the Holy Spirit to bring up any memories of your abortion: perhaps of the day you discovered you were pregnant; the reactions of the child's father or your parents; the feeling of abandonment; the dilemma of making the decision to go to the abortion clinic; the actual procedure; the days following the abortion; or any other memories or flashbacks you find troubling. Write what comes back to you here:

_____

_____

_____

_____

_____

_____

_____

_____

_____

Do the Divine Exchange. As a memory comes back to your mind, ask Jesus to come into the memory. Then wait, and expect to see Jesus in the midst of your memory. Now simply allow yourself to feel the pain and then give it to Jesus. What is Jesus doing now? Is He reaching out His hands to you, hugging you, or maybe drying your tears? Say to Jesus, *"Please heal this memory so that it no longer keeps me chained."* Finally, listen to what Jesus says to you and write it down.

_____

_____

_____

Receive His peace. Jesus bore the pain of this memory when He died on the cross. Say, *Thank you risen Lord for You have healed my memory."* Don't rush. Let the tears flow. Crying is healing. Psalm 126:5 says "May those who sow in tears reap with shouts of joy".

And don't worry if you can't see Jesus in your mind or hear Him say anything. Not everyone does. But trust that Jesus is with you. He sees you, and He hears the cries of your heart. Jesus is holding you. He's crying with you. Jesus is feeling your distress. He's receiving all your pain upon Himself. Jesus is healing you.

Healing of Grief
Ask the Holy Spirit to help you identify your losses. Then write them down here.

_____

_____

_____

Talk to Jesus about your grief and your pain. Jesus is the Healer. He is listening and is right there with you. When you are ready, say, *"Jesus, I give You my grief and my pain. Thank You for receiving all my pain and grief."*

Turn to Jesus and pray, *"Jesus, just like the woman in the Scriptures, I reach out my hand to touch the hem of Your cloak. I ask for the healing power that flows from Your cross and resurrection to flow through my body and to heal me of these physical or emotional conditions related to my abortion* (name them)."

Take a moment to hear Jesus say, "I am always with you, _____(insert name)_____." If you have any memories of people letting you down, lying to you, or just not being there for you— especially regarding your abortion—stop for a few minutes. Ask Jesus to forgive you for any anger or resentment you still feel. Then follow the steps in the previous reflection for the healing of memories because Jesus is your Healer.

Pray now with great expectancy, *"Holy Spirit, come and baptize me with the fire of Your love."* Don't rush. Sit for five or ten minutes, and allow the Holy Spirit to minister to you in whatever way He chooses. Perhaps you will experience a special sense of His presence. Perhaps a word or thought you know is not your own or a few words from a Scripture verse will pop into your head. Or perhaps you will see a picture in your mind. Whatever it is, it will be something very personal, just for you! Write about this time of prayer in your journal.

_____

_____

_____

Holy Spirit wants to replace them with these Truths. Please repeat them after me:

- My child is a beloved son/daughter of God (Psalm 139).
- My child is in heaven – I am his/her mother (Genesis 1:27).
- I am forgiven for aborting my child. My sin is redeemed (Colossians 1:13-14).
- I can, with confidence, entrust my child to the Lord (Luke 12:7).
-

Here's one more thought about your child: why not choose a name for your child? Remember! You hope to be living with your child in the presence of the Lord for all of eternity.

Say to your child, "I am naming you _____ !" Enjoy this time thinking about your child. Receive all the inner healing that the Holy Spirit is doing in your life right now. Remember this is a journey and there are layers of pain for Jesus to heal. Holy Spirit loves you and wants to fill you with His awesome transforming power. What you believe, you will receive!

 **Sample Prayer**

Healing Process and Prayer for Men Who Aborted a Child
"Lord my God, I cried to You for help, and You healed me." (Psalm 30:2)

Begin by praying, *"Jesus, I don't want to be chained any longer by memories of my abortion decision. Please come and heal me."* Now ask the Holy Spirit to bring up any memories of the abortion decision: perhaps of the day you discovered your partner was pregnant; the reactions of your partner or your parents; feelings of resentment or anger; the dilemma of making the decision to go to the abortion clinic; the day of the actual procedure; the days following the abortion; or any other memories or flashbacks you find troubling.

As a memory comes back to your mind, ask Jesus to come into the memory. Then wait, and expect to see Jesus in the midst of your memory. Now simply allow yourself to feel the pain. What is Jesus doing now? Is He reaching out His hands to you, hugging you, or maybe drying your tears? Say to Jesus, *"Please heal this memory so that it no longer keeps me chained."*

Finally, listen to what Jesus says to you. Perhaps He is saying, "I was there all the time with you. Receive My peace. I bore the pain of this memory when I died on the cross. I'm your risen Lord. I have healed your memory." Don't rush. If there are tears, allow them to flow. Crying is healing. *"May those who sow in tears reap with shouts of joy"* (Psalm 126:5).

Ask Holy Spirit to help you identify your losses. Then write them down:

_____

_____

_____

What is grief? Grief is a deep sorrow and sadness. Grief is painful and emotionally exhausting. Grief can leave a person feeling empty and numb. And grief is normal after a loss. So give yourself permission to grieve the loss or losses you've identified. Don't be afraid to feel the grief and the pain of your losses. Your grief is real. And your pain is real. But if you allow yourself to heal, the pain you are feeling now will diminish over time.

Do the Divine Exchange: Talk to Jesus about your grief and your pain. Jesus is the Healer. He is listening and is right there with you. When you are ready, say, *"Jesus, I give You my grief and my pain. Please take it all."*

Spend some time in prayer with your eyes closed, and ask God your Father to come in and heal this wound of shame in your heart. Identify the pain in your heart or wherever you feel it, and ask God to place His healing hand upon you, and to come in and heal that pain. He desires to do this. You may want to repeat this prayer during your journey to healing as God your Father heals your wound.

From: https://waupartners.org/resources/article/after_abortion_forgiveness_ healing_and_hope

Breaking the Unhealthy Soul Tie of Rape and Incest Prayer

Father, I have suffered as an unwilling victim of incest. Therefore, I re-nounce and break the family spirit of incest and rape. I break the family spirit of rape off my body, emotions and finances. I break the depression and grief of rape. I ask that Holy Spirit will heal my wounds. I break every dimension of death that comes with rape in the name of Jesus. Where the spirit of incest with rape has caused me to have fear, I break the fear of rape. I break the paranoia, mistrust and suspicion that comes with fear of rape. I ask You Father, to restore my sense of proportion, truth and reality.

I repent where I have been tied through spiritual incest with a fam-ily member, or even an unhealthy soul tie with a 'sister' or 'brother' in church. I break the bondage of incest. I revoke the covenant of spiritual incest between them and me in the name of Jesus. I break the lust for possessive ownership of another. I repent for having defiled the Body of Christ with spiritual incest.

I repent where another and I are bound by cords of spiritual incest and where we have become connected in emotions and in spirit, I repent. I take the sword of the spirit and separate myself from every ungodly soul tie through the incest spirit that binds us together. I break the spirit of incest that joins another and myself. I break the spirit of torment and insanity that comes as a result of incestuous relationships.

They _____(perpetrator)_____are free and I am free of all soul ties in the powerful name of Jesus. And by His stripes I am healed of any mental or physical afflictions due to incest. Amen.

Personal Notes

_____

_____

_____

_____

_____

_____

_____

_____

_____

_____

_____

_____

_____

_____

_____

_____

_____

_____

_____

_____

_____

Protection Prayers if You're Struggling

Midnight Prayers by Dr. D.K. Olukoya
Make These Declarations Out Loud and Pray Them One by One
I use this comprehensive prayer if I'm feeling attacked in any way. This is also helpful if you are experiencing bad dreams.

I put on the full armor of God now in Jesus name according to Ephesians 6:10-18:
- The belt of truth
- The breastplate of righteousness
- The helmet of salvation
- The shoes of peace
- The shield of faith
- The sword of the Spirit

I position myself in the spiritual realm and call upon the Lord of Hosts and His Angels of Deliverance to minister on my behalf in Jesus name.

I soak my spirit soul and body in the blood of Jesus Christ and declare that this is the day of my great deliverance, healing and breakthrough by fire and by force in Jesus name.

I close every door by the blood of Jesus that was opened by me knowingly or unknowingly that might hinder my prayers. I close it now in Jesus name.

Midnight Declarations

1. **Now touch your head and repeat this several times (x 12) until you can feel a release:** Jesus Christ of Nazareth baptize me now with the Holy Ghost and fire in Jesus name.

2. Every strange spirit attacking my life; be destroyed now by fire

in Jesus name.

3. Family Imprints and strongholds, curses and the strongman of my father's house let me loose now by fire in Jesus name.

4. **Touch your naval/stomach as you pray this prayer:**
I cut and disconnect myself from any spiritual cord that is connecting me to demonic foundations, marine* altars and human spirits; I cut it now with the sword of the Spirit by fire in Jesus name.

5. I break the spirit of poverty and command every blessing that belongs to me; to be vomited now by the marine serpent in Jesus name.

6. I disconnect myself from marine altars and demonic dreams; I disconnect my life from their influence in Jesus name.

7. I destroy the spiritual wife/husband assigned to destroy my life; I arrest them now by fire in Jesus name.

8. I renounce every involvement in the demonic kingdom that I have ever entered into.

9. I destroy every contract binding my destiny in Jesus name.

10. I call down fire upon every assembly of the kingdom of darkness assigned to destroy me. Let fire consume them now in Jesus name.

11. I receive total deliverance from demonic covenants.

12. I shall live and not die to proclaim the glory of God.

13. Every evil monitoring spirit, monitoring my progress; be arrested now by fire in Jesus name.

14. Enemies of progress against my success be paralyzed by fire and die in Jesus name.

15. I take all my riches, gifts and blessings held up by the serpent in Jesus name.

16. I take my prayer life back in Jesus name.

17. Holy Ghost fire, purge my life completely in Jesus name.

18. I claim my complete deliverance in the name of Jesus Christ from all domestic demonic covenants in Jesus mighty name.

19. **Lay your hand on your head and another on your stomach and begin to pray this:** Holy Ghost fire, burn from the top of my head to the sole of my feet now in Jesus name.

20. I accelerate from bondage to freedom in every area of my life in Jesus name.

21. I command every evil plantation in my life: Come out now by fire with all your roots in Jesus mighty name.

22. Every evil stranger in my body I cast you out now by fire in Jesus mighty name.

23. **Begin to touch your head, neck, chest, stomach, etc. and keep repeating this prayer:** I take all authority and legal rights back in Jesus mighty name.

Give thanks and have a goodnight's rest!

Free Masonry Prayer of Renunciation

 I strongly encourage you to read through this prayer as instructed below. It's the most comprehensive Free Masonry Prayer of Renunciation that I've found and it's extremely effective in cutting off the many family imprints that come from freemasonry. In addition to being the world's oldest fraternal organization, Freemasonry is also the world's largest such organization, boasting an estimated worldwide membership of some 6 million people, according to a report by the BBC. Therefore, you may have freemasonry in your lineage. Regardless of your ancestry, it doesn't hurt to read this.

Please pray this outloud with someone. We suggest a brief pause following each paragraph to allow the Holy Spirit to show any related issues which may require attention.

A significant number of people also reported having experienced physical and spiritual healings as diverse as long-term headaches and epilepsy as the result of praying through this prayer. Christian counsellors and pastors in many countries have been using this prayer in counselling situations and seminars for several years, with real and significant results.

Some language could be described as 'quaint Old English' and are the real terms used in the Masonic ritual. The legal renunciation opens the way for spiritual, emotional and physical healing to take place.

There are differences between British Commonwealth Masonry and American & Prince Hall Masonry in the higher degrees. Degrees unique to Americans are marked with this sign "" at the commencement of each paragraph. Those of British Commonwealth descent shouldn't need to pray through those paragraphs.*

The Prayer of Release

Father God, creator of heaven and earth, I come to you in the name of Jesus Christ your Son. I come as a sinner seeking forgiveness and cleansing from all sins committed against you, and others made in your image. I honour my earthly father and mother and all of my ancestors of flesh and blood, and of the spirit by adoption and god-parents, but I utterly turn away from and renounce all their sins. I forgive all my ancestors for the effects of their sins on me and my children. I confess and renounce all of my own sins, known and unknown. I renounce and rebuke Satan and every spiritual power of his affecting me and my family, in the name of Jesus Christ.

True Holy Creator God, in the name of the True Lord Jesus Christ, in accordance with Jude 8-10; Psalm 82:1 and 2 Chronicles 18, I request you to move aside all Celestial Beings, including Principalities, Powers and Rulers, and to forbid them to harass, intimidate or retaliate against me and all participants in this ministry today.

I also ask that you prevent and forbid these beings, of whatever rank, from sending any level of spiritual evil as retaliation against any of those here, or our families, our ministries, or possessions.

I renounce and annul every covenant made with Death by my ancestors or myself, including every agreement made with Sheol, and I renounce the refuge of lies and falsehoods which have been hidden behind.

In the name of the Lord Jesus Christ, I renounce and forsake all involvement in Freemasonry or any other lodge, craft or occultism by my ancestors and myself. I also renounce and break the code of silence enforced by Freemasonry and the Occult on my family and myself. I renounce and repent of all pride and arrogance which opened the door for the slavery and bondage of Freemasonry to afflict my family and me. I now shut every door of witchcraft and deception operating in my life and seal it closed with the blood of the Lord Jesus Christ. I renounce every covenant, every blood covenant and every alliance with Freemasonry or the spiritual powers behind it made by my family or me.

In the name of Jesus Christ, I rebuke, renounce and bind Witchcraft, the principal spirit behind Freemasonry, and I renounce and rebuke Baphomet, the Spirit of Antichrist and the spirits of Death, and Deception.

I renounce and rebuke the Spirit of Fides, the Roman goddess of Fidelity that seeks to hold all Masonic and occultic participants and their descendants in bondage, and I ask the One True Holy Creator God to give me the gift of Faith to believe in the True Lord Jesus Christ as described in the Word of God.

I also renounce and rebuke the Spirit of Prostitution which the Word of God says has led members of Masonic and other Occultic organisations astray, and caused them to become unfaithful to the One True and Holy God. I now choose to return and become faithful to the God of the Bible, the God of Abraham, Isaac and Jacob, the Father of Jesus Christ, who I now declare is my Lord and Saviour.

I renounce the insecurity, the love of position and power, the love of money, avarice or greed, and the pride which would have led my ancestors into Masonry. I renounce all the fears which held them in Masonry, especially the fears of death, fears of men, and fears of trusting, in the name of Jesus Christ.

I renounce every position held in the lodge by any of my ancestors or myself, including "Master," "Worshipful Master," or any other occultic title. I renounce the calling of any man "Master," for Jesus Christ is my only master and Lord, and He forbids anyone else having that title. I renounce the entrapping of others into Masonry, and observing the helplessness of others during the rituals. I renounce the effects of Masonry passed on to me through any female ancestor who felt distrusted and rejected by her husband as he entered and attended any lodge and refused to tell her of his secret activities. I also renounce all obligations, oaths and curses enacted by every female member of my family through any direct membership of all Women's Orders of Freemasonry, the Order of the Eastern Star, or any other Masonic or occultic organisation.

All participants should now be invited to sincerely carry out in faith the following actions:

1. Symbolically remove the blindfold (hoodwink) and give it to the Lord for disposal;
2. In the same way, symbolically remove the veil of mourning, to make way to receive the Joy of the Lord:
3. Symbolically cut and remove the noose from around the neck, gather it up with the cabletow running down the body and give it all to the Lord for His disposal;
4. Renounce the false Freemasonry marriage covenant, removing from the 4th finger of the right hand the ring of this false marriage covenant, giving it to the Lord to dispose of it;
5. Symbolically remove the chains and bondages of Freemasonry from your body;
6. Symbolically remove all Freemasonry regalia, including collars, gauntlets and armour, especially the Apron with its snake clasp, to make way for the Belt of Truth;
7. Remove the slipshod slippers, to make way for the shoes of the Gospel of Peace;
8. Symbolically remove the ball and chain from the ankles.
9. Invite participants to repent of and seek forgiveness for having walked on all unholy ground, including Freemasonry lodges and temples, including any Mormon or any other occultic/Masonic organisations.
10. Proclaim that Satan and his demons no longer have any legal rights to mislead and manipulate the person seeking help.

33rd & Supreme Degree

In the name of Jesus Christ I renounce the oaths taken and the curses and iniquities involved in the supreme Thirty-Third Degree of Freemasonry, the Grand Sovereign Inspector General. I renounce the secret passwords, DEMOLAY-HIRUM ABIFF, FREDERICK OF PRUSSIA, MICHA, MACHA, BEALIM, and ADONAI, and all their occultic and Masonic meanings. I renounce all of the obligations of every Masonic degree, and all penalties invoked.

I renounce and utterly forsake The Great Architect Of The Universe, who is revealed in the this degree as Lucifer, and his false claim to be the universal fatherhood of God. I reject the Masonic view of deity because it does not square with the revelation of the One True and Holy Creator God of the Bible.

I renounce the cable-tow around the neck. I renounce the death wish that the wine drunk from a human skull should turn to poison and the skeleton whose cold arms are invited if the oath of this degree is violated. I renounce the three infamous assassins of their grand master, law, property and religion, and the greed and witchcraft involved in the attempt to manipulate and control the rest of mankind.

In the name of God the Father, Jesus Christ the Son, and the Holy Spirit, I renounce and break the curses and iniquities involved in the idolatry, blasphemy, secrecy and deception of Freemasonry at every level, and I appropriate the Blood of Jesus Christ to cleanse all the consequences of these from my life. I now revoke all previous consent given by any of my ancestors or myself to be deceived.

Blue Lodge
In the name of Jesus Christ I renounce the oaths taken and the curses and iniquities involved in the First or Entered Apprentice Degree, especially their effects on the throat and tongue. I renounce the Hoodwink blindfold and its effects on spirit, emotions and eyes, including all confusion, fear of the dark, fear of the light, and fear of sudden noises. I renounce the blinding of spiritual truth, the darkness of the soul, the false imagination, condescension and the spirit of poverty caused by the ritual of this degree. I also renounce the usurping of the marriage covenant by the removal of the wedding ring. I renounce the secret word, BOAZ, and it's Masonic meaning. I renounce the serpent clasp on the apron, and the spirit of Python which it brought to squeeze the spiritual life out of me.

I renounce the ancient pagan teaching from Babylon and Egypt and the symbolism of the First Tracing Board. I renounce the mixing and mingling of truth and error, the mythology, fabrications and lies taught as truth, and the dishonesty by leaders as to the true understanding of the ritual, and the blasphemy of this degree of Freemasonry.

I renounce the breaking of five of God's Ten Commandments during participation in the rituals of the Blue Lodge degrees. I renounce the presentation to every compass direction, for all the Earth is the Lord's, and everything in it. I renounce the cabletow noose around the neck, the fear of choking and also every spirit causing asthma, hayfever, emphysema or any other breathing difficulty. I renounce the ritual dagger, or the compass point, sword or spear held against the breast, the fear of death by stabbing pain, and the fear of heart attack from this degree, and the absolute secrecy demanded under a witchcraft oath and sealed by kissing the Volume of the Sacred Law. I also renounce kneeling to the false deity known as the Great Architect of the Universe, and humbly ask the One True God to forgive me for this idolatry, in the name of Jesus Christ.

I renounce the pride of proven character and good standing required prior to joining Freemasonry, and the resulting self-righteousness of being good enough to stand before God without the need of a saviour. I now pray for healing of… (throat, vocal cords, nasal passages, sinus, bronchial tubes etc.) for healing of the speech area, and the release of the Word of God to me and through me and my family.

Second or Fellow Craft Degree of Masonry
In the name of Jesus Christ I renounce the oaths taken and the curses and iniquities involved in the Second or Fellow Craft Degree of Masonry, especially the curses on the heart and chest. I renounce the secret words SHIBBOLETH and JACHIN, and all their Masonic meaning. I renounce the ancient pagan teaching and symbolism of the Second Tracing Board. I renounce the Sign of Reverence to the Generative Principle. I cut off emotional hardness, apathy, indifference, unbelief, and deep anger from me and my family. In the name of Jesus' Christ I pray for the healing of …(the chest/lung/heart area) and also for the healing of my emotions, and ask to be made sensitive to the Holy Spirit of God.

Third or Master Mason Degree
In the name of Jesus Christ I renounce the oaths taken and the curses and iniquities involved in the Third or Master Mason Degree, especially the curses on the stomach and womb area. I renounce the secret words TUBAL CAIN and MAHA BONE, and all their Masonic meaning. I renounce the ancient pagan teaching and symbolism of the Third Tracing Board used in the ritual. I renounce the Spirit of Death from the blows to the head enacted as ritual murder, the fear of death, false martyrdom, fear of violent gang attack, assault, or rape, and the helplessness of this degree. I renounce the falling into the coffin or stretcher involved in the ritual of murder.

In the name of Jesus Christ I renounce Hiram Abiff, the false saviour of Freemasons revealed in this degree. I renounce the false resurrection of this degree, because only Jesus Christ is the Resurrection and the Life!

I renounce the pagan ritual of the "Point within a Circle" with all its bondages and phallus worship. I renounce the symbol "G" and its veiled pagan symbolism and bondages. I renounce the occultic mysticism of the black and white mosaic chequered floor with the tessellated boarder and five-pointed blazing star.

I renounce the All-Seeing Third Eye of Freemasonry or Horus in the forehead and its pagan and occult symbolism. I rebuke and reject every spirit of divination which allowed this occult ability to operate. Action: Put your hand over your forehead.) I now close that Third eye and all occult ability to see into the spiritual realm, in the name of the Lord Jesus Christ, and put my trust in the Holy Spirit sent by Jesus Christ for all I need to know on spiritual matters. I renounce all false communions taken, all mockery of the redemptive work of Jesus Christ on the cross of Calvary, all unbelief, confusion and depression. I renounce and forsake the lie of Freemasonry that man is not sinful, but merely imperfect, and so can redeem himself through good works. I rejoice that the Bible states that I cannot do a single thing to earn my salvation, but that I can only be saved by grace through faith in Jesus Christ and what He accomplished on the Cross of Calvary.

I renounce all fear of insanity, anguish, death wishes, suicide and death in the name of Jesus Christ. Death was conquered by Jesus Christ, and He alone holds the keys of death and hell, and I rejoice that He holds my life in His hands now. He came to give me life abundantly and eternally, and I believe His promises.

I renounce all anger, hatred, murderous thoughts, revenge, retaliation, spiritual apathy, false religion, all unbelief, especially unbelief in the Holy Bible as God's Word, and all compromise of God's Word. I renounce all spiritual searching into false religions, and all striving to please God. I rest in the knowledge that I have found my Lord and Saviour Jesus Christ, and that He has found me.

In the name of Jesus Christ I pray for the healing of… (the stomach, gall bladder, womb, liver, and any other organs of my body affected by Masonry), and I ask for a release of compassion and understanding for me and my family.

York Rite
I renounce and forsake the oaths taken and the curses and iniquities involved in the York Rite Degrees of Masonry. I renounce the Mark Lodge, and the mark in the form of squares and angles which marks the person for life. I also reject the jewel or occult talisman which may have been made from this mark sign and worn at lodge meetings; <br.
the Mark Master Degree with its secret word JOPPA, and its penalty of having the right ear smote off and the curse of permanent deafness, as well as the right hand being chopped off for being an imposter.

I also renounce and forsake the oaths taken and the curses and iniquities involved in the other York Rite Degrees, including Past Master, with the penalty of having my tongue split from tip to root; <br. and of the Most Excellent Master Degree, in which the penalty is to have my breast torn open and my heart and vital organs removed and exposed to rot on the dung hill.

Holy Royal Arch Degree
In the name of Jesus Christ, I renounce and forsake the oaths taken and the curses and iniquities involved in the Holy Royal Arch Degree especially the oath regarding the removal of the head from the body and the exposing of the brains to the hot sun. I renounce the false secret name of God, JAHBULON, and declare total rejection of all worship of the false pagan gods, Bul or Baal, and On or Osiris. I also renounce the password, AMMI RUHAMAH and all it's Masonic meaning. I renounce the false communion or Eucharist taken in this degree, and all the mockery, scepticism and unbelief about the redemptive work of Jesus Christ on the cross of Calvary. I cut off all these curses and their effects on me and my family in the name of Jesus Christ, and I pray for... (healing of the brain, the mind etc.)

I renounce and forsake the oaths taken and the curses and iniquities involved in the Royal Master Degree of the York Rite; the Select Master Degree with its penalty to have my hands chopped off to the stumps, to have my eyes plucked out from their sockets, and to have my body quartered and thrown among the rubbish of the Temple.

I renounce and forsake the oaths taken and the curses and iniqui-ties involved in the Super Excellent Master Degree along with the penalty of having my thumbs cut off, my eyes put out, my body bound in fetters and brass, and conveyed captive to a strange land; and also of the Knights or Illustrious Order of the Red Cross, along with the penalty of having my house torn down and my be-ing hanged on the exposed timbers.

I renounce the Knights Templar Degree and the secret words of KEB RAIOTH, and also Knights of Malta Degree and the secret words MAHER-SHALAL-HASH-BAZ.

I renounce the vows taken on a human skull, the crossed swords, and the curse and death wish of Judas of having the head cut off and placed on top of a church spire. I renounce the unholy com-munion and especially of drinking from a human skull in many Rites.

Ancient & Accepted or Scottish Rite
(Only the 18th, 30th, 31st 32nd & 33rd degree are operated in British Commonwealth countries.)
*** * I renounce the oaths taken and the curses, iniquities and penalties involved in the American and Grand Orient Lodges, in-cluding of the Secret Master Degree, its secret passwords of ADO-NAI and ZIZA, and their occult meanings. I reject and renounce the worship of the pagan sun god as the Great Source of Light, and the crowning with laurel – sacred to Apollo, and the sign of secrecy in obedience to Horus;

*** of the Perfect Master Degree, its secret password of MAH-HAH-BONE, and its penalty of being smitten to the Earth with a setting maul;

*** * of the Intimate Secretary Degree, its secret passwords of YEVA and JOABERT, and its penalties of having my body dissected, and of having my vital organs cut into pieces and thrown to the beasts of the field, and of the use of the nine-pointed star from the Kab-bala and the worship of Phallic energy;

*** of the Provost and Judge Degree, its secret password of HIRUM-TITO-CIVI-KY, and the penalty of having my nose cut off;

*** of the Intendant of the Building Degree, of its secret password

AKAR-JAI-JAH, and the penalty of having my eyes put out, my body cut in two and exposing my bowels;

*** of the Elected Knights of the Nine Degree, its secret password NEKAM NAKAH, and its penalty of having my head cut off and stuck on the highest pole in the East;

*** of the Illustrious Elect of Fifteen Degree, with its secret password ELIGNAM, and its penalties of having my body opened perpendicularly and horizontally, the entrails exposed to the air for eight hours so that flies may prey on them, and for my head to be cut off and placed on a high pinnacle;

*** of the Sublime Knights elect of the Twelve Degree, its secret password STOLKIN-ADONAI, and its penalty of having my hand cut in twain;

*** of the Grand Master Architect Degree, its secret password RAB-BANAIM, and its penalties;

*** * of the Knight of the Ninth Arch of Solomon or Enoch Degree, its secret password JEHOVAH, it's blasphemous use, its penalty of having my body given to the beasts of the forest as prey, and I also renounce the revelations from the Kabbala in this and subsequent degrees;

*** * of the Grand Elect, Perfect and Sublime Mason or Elu Degree, its secret password MARAH-MAUR-ABREK and IHUH, the penalty of having my body cut open and my bowels given to vultures for food, and I reject the Great Unknowable deity of this degree;

Council of Princes of Jerusalem
*** of the Knights of the East Degree, its secret password RAPH-O-DOM, and its penalties;

*** of the Prince of Jerusalem Degree, its secret password TEBET-ADAR, and its penalty of being stripped naked and having my heart pierced with a ritual dagger;

Chapter of the Rose Croix
*** * of the Knight of the East and West Degree, its secret password ABADDON, and its penalty of incurring the severe wrath of the Almighty Creator of Heaven and Earth. I also reject the Tet-

ractys and its representation of the Sephiroth from the Kabbala and its false tree of life. I also reject the false anointing with oil and the proclamation that anyone so anointed is now worthy to open the Book of Seven Seals, because only the Lord Jesus Christ is worthy;

18th Degree

I renounce the oaths taken and the curses, iniquities and penalties involved in the Eighteenth Degree of Freemasonry, the Most Wise Sovereign Knight of the Pelican and the Eagle and Sovereign Prince Rose Croix of Heredom. I renounce and reject the false Jesus revealed in this degree because He doesn't point to the light or the truth since the True Lord Jesus Christ is the Light of the World and the Truth. I renounce and reject the Pelican witchcraft spirit, as well as the occultic influence of the Rosicrucians and the Kabbala in this degree.

I renounce the claim that the death of Jesus Christ was a "dire calamity," and also the deliberate mockery and twisting of the Christian doctrine of the Atonement. I renounce the blasphemy and rejection of the deity of Jesus Christ, and the secret words IGNE NATURA RENOVATUR INTEGRA and its burning. I renounce the mockery of the communion taken in this degree, including a biscuit, salt and white wine.

Council of Kadosh

*** I renounce the inappropriate use of the title "Kadosh" used in these council degrees because it means "Holy" and it is here used in a unholy way.

I renounce the oaths taken and the curses, iniquities and penalties involved in the Grand Pontiff Degree, its secret password EMMANUEL, and its penalties;

*** * of the Grand Master of Symbolic Lodges or Ad Vitum Degree, its secret passwords JEKSON and STOLKIN, and the penalties invoked, and I also reject the pagan Phoenecian and Hindu deities revealed in this degree;

*** * of the Patriarch Noachite or Prussian Knight Degree, its secret password PELEG, and its penalties;

*** * of the Knight of the Royal Axe or Prince of Libanus Degree, its secret password NOAH-BEZALEEL-SODONIAS, and its penalties;

*** * of the Chief of the Tabernacle Degree, its secret password URIEL-JEHOVAH, and its penalty that I agree the Earth should open up and engulf me up to my neck so I perish, and I also reject the false title of becoming a "Son of Light" in this degree;

*** * of the Prince of the Tabernacle Degree, and its penalty to be stoned to death and have my body left above ground to rot. I also reject the claimed revelation of the mysteries of the Hebrew faith from the Kabbala, and the occultic and pagan Egyptian, Hindu, Mithraic, Dionysian and Orphic mysteries revealed and worshipped in this degree;

*** * of the Knight of the Brazen Serpent Degree, its secret password MOSES-JOHANNES, and its penalty to have my heart eaten by venomous serpents. I also reject the claimed revelation of the mysteries of the Islamic faith, I reject the insulting misquotations from the Koran, and the gift of a white turban in this degree;

*** * of the Prince of Mercy Degree, its secret password GOMEL, JEHOVAH-JACHIN, and its penalty of condemnation and spite by the entire universe. I also reject the claimed revelation of the mysteries of the Christian religion because there are no such mysteries. I reject the Druid trinity of Odin, Frea and Thor revealed in this degree. I also reject the false baptism claimed for the purification of my soul to allow my soul to rejoin the universal soul of Buddhism, as taught in this degree;

*** * of the Knight Commander of the Temple Degree, its secret password SOLOMON, and its penalty of receiving the severest wrath of Almighty God inflicted upon me. I also reject the claimed revelation of the mysteries of Numerology, Astrology and Alchemy and other occult sciences taught in this degree;

*** * of the Knight Commander of the Sun, or Prince Adept Degree, its secret password STIBIUM, and its penalties of having my tongue thrust through with a red-hot iron, of my eyes being plucked out, of my senses of smelling and hearing being removed, of having my hands cut off and in that condition to be left for voracious animals to devour me, or executed by lightning from heaven;

*** * of the Grand Scottish Knight of Saint Andrew or Patriarch of the Crusades Degree, its secret password NEKAMAH-FURLAC, and its penalties;

Thirtieth Degree
I renounce the oaths taken and the curses and iniquities involved in the Thirtieth Degree of Masonry, the Grand Knight Kadosh and Knight of the Black and White Eagle. I renounce the secret passwords, STIBIUM ALKABAR, PHARASH-KOH and all they mean.

Sublime Princes of The Royal Secret
Thirty-First Degree of Masonry
I renounce the oaths taken and the curses and iniquities involved in the Thirty-First Degree of Masonry, the Grand Inspector Inquisitor Commander. I renounce all the gods and goddesses of Egypt which are honoured in this degree, including Anubis with the jackel's head, Osiris the Sun god, Isis the sister and wife of Osiris and also the moon goddess. I renounce the Soul of Cheres, the false symbol of immortality, the Chamber of the dead and the false teaching of reincarnation.

Thirty-Second Degree of Masonry
I renounce the oaths taken and the curses and iniquities involved in the Thirty-Second Degree of Masonry, the Sublime Prince of the Royal Secret. I renounce the secret passwords, PHAAL/PHARASH-KOL and all they mean. I renounce Masonry's false trinitarian deity AUM, and its parts; Brahma the creator, Vishnu the preserver and Shiva the destroyer. I renounce the deity of AHURA-MAZDA, the claimed spirit or source of all light, and the worship with fire, which is an abomination to God, and also the drinking from a human skull in many Rites.

Shriners (Applies only in North America)
*** I renounce the oaths taken and the curses, iniquities and penalties involved in the Ancient Arabic Order of the Nobles of the Mystic Shrine. I renounce the piercing of the eyeballs with a three-edged blade, the flaying of the feet, the madness, and the worship of the false god Allah as the god of our fathers. I renounce the hoodwink, the mock hanging, the mock beheading, the mock drinking of the blood of the victim, the mock dog urinating on the initiate, and the offering of urine as a commemoration.

All Other Degrees

I renounce all the other oaths taken, the rituals of every other degree and the curses and iniquities invoked. These include the Acacia, Allied Degrees, The Red Cross of Constantine, the Order of the Secret Monitor, and the Masonic Royal Order of Scotland.

I renounce all other lodges and secret societies including Prince Hall Freemasonry, Grand Orient Lodges, Mormonism, the Ancient Toltec Rite, The Order of Amaranth, the Royal Order of Jesters, the Manchester Unity Order of Oddfellows and its womens' Order of Rebekah lodges, the Royal Antediluvian Order of Buffaloes, Druids, Foresters, the Loyal Order of Orange, including the Purple and Black Lodges within it, Elks, Moose and Eagles Lodges, the Ku Klux Klan, The Grange, the Woodmen of the World, Riders of the Red Robe, the Knights of Pythias, the Order of the Builders, The Rite of Memphiz and Mitzraim, Ordo Templi Orientis (OTO), Aleister Crowley's Palladium Masonry, the Order of the Golden Key, the Order of Desoms, the Mystic Order of the Veiled Prophets of the Enchanted Realm, the women's Orders of the Eastern Star, of the Ladies Oriental Shrine, and of the White Shrine of Jerusalem, the girls' order of the Daughters of the Eastern Star, the International Orders of Job's Daughters, and of the Rainbow, the boys' Order of De Molay, and the Order of the Constellation of Junior Stars, and every university or college Fraternity or Sorority with Greek and Masonic connections, and their effects on me and all my family.

Lord Jesus, because you want me to be totally free from all occult bondages, I will burn all objects in my possession which connect me with all lodges and occultic organisations, including Masonry, Witchcraft, the Occult and Mormonism, and all regalia, aprons, books of rituals, rings and other jewellery. I renounce the effects these or other objects of Masonry, including the compass and the square, have had on me or my family, in the name of Jesus Christ.

In the name and authority of Jesus Christ, I break every curse of Freemasonry in my life, including the curses of barrenness, sickness, mind-blinding and poverty, and I rebuke every evil spirit which empowered these curses.

I also renounce, cut off and dissolve in the blood of Jesus Christ every ungodly Soul-Tie I or my ancestors have created with other lodge members or participants in occultic groups and actions, and I ask you to send out ministering angels to gather together all portions of my fragmented soul, to free them from all bondages and to wash them clean in the Blood of Jesus Christ, and then to restore them to wholeness to their rightful place within me. I also ask that You remove from me any parts of any other person's soul which has been deposited within my humanity. Thank you Lord for restoring my soul and sanctifying my spirit.

I renounce and rebuke every evil spirit associated with Freemasonry, Witchcraft , the Occult and all other sins and iniquities. Lord Jesus, I ask you to now set me free from all spiritual and other bondages, in accordance with the many promises of the Bible.

In the name of the Lord Jesus Christ, I now take the delegated authority given to me and bind every spirit of sickness, infirmity, curse, affliction, addiction, disease or allergy associated with these sins I have confessed and renounced, including every spirit empowering all iniquities inherited from my family. I exercise the delegated authority from the Risen Lord Jesus Christ over all lower levels of evil spirits and demons which have been assigned to me, and I command that all such demonic beings are to be bound up into one, to be separated from every part of my humanity, whether perceived to be in the body or trapped in the dimensions, and they are not permitted to transfer power to any other spirits or to call for reinforcements.

I command, in the name of Jesus Christ, for every evil spirit to leave me now, touching or harming no-one, and go to the dry place appointed for you by the Lord Jesus Christ, never to return to me or my family, and I command that you now take all your memories, roots, scars, works, nests and habits with you. I surrender to God's Holy Spirit and to no other spirit all the places in my life where these sins and iniquities have been.

Conclusion
Holy Spirit, I ask that you show me anything else which I need to do or to pray so that I and my family may be totally free from the consequences of the sins of Masonry, Witchcraft, Mormonism and all related Paganism and Occultism.
(Pause, while listening to God, and pray as the Holy Spirit leads you.)
Now, dear Father God, I ask humbly for the blood of Jesus Christ, your Son and my Saviour, to cleanse me from all these sins I have

confessed and renounced, to cleanse my spirit, my soul, my mind, my emotions and every part of my body which has been affected by these sins, in the name of Jesus Christ. I also command every cell in my body to come into divine order now, and to be healed and made whole as they were designed to by my loving Creator, including restoring all chemical balances and neurological functions, controlling all cancerous cells, reversing all degenerative diseases, and I sever the DNA and RNA of any mental or physical diseases or afflictions that came down through my family blood lines. I also ask to receive the perfect love of God which casts out all fear, in the name of the Lord Jesus Christ.

I ask you, Lord, to fill me with your Holy Spirit now according to the promises in your Word. I take to myself the whole armour of God in accordance with Ephesians Chapter Six, and rejoice in its protection as Jesus surrounds me and fills me with His Holy Spirit. I enthrone you, Lord Jesus, in my heart, for you are my Lord and my Saviour, the source of eternal life. Thank you, Father God, for your mercy, your forgiveness and your love, in the name of Jesus Christ, Amen."

Since the above is what needs to be renounced, why would anyone want to join?

This information is taken from *Unmasking Freemasonry – Removing the Hoodwink*, (ISBN 978-1877463-00-6) by Dr. Selwyn Stevens published by Jubilee Resource International Inc., PO Box 36-044, Wellington Mail Centre 5045, New Zealand.

Notice Copying of this prayer is both permitted and encouraged provided reference is made to Book title, Author, Publisher & web address – www.jubilee-resources.com. This and other similar prayers are available to download freely from our website. Resources on other subjects are also available to educate and equip Christians on a wide range of spiritual deceptions. These prayers are also in Spanish, Brazilian Portuguese, French, German and Italian, and other languages as can be arranged.

Bonus Lessons

Who Owns this Problem?

Your job is to own your own problems and not own other people's problems. Too often we focus on helping or controlling other people so that we don't have to confront our own issues. Identifying one's own problems leads to the healing of root issues in your life.

1. What is "Problem Ownership"?

> *"Bear each other's burdens (Greek "baros"), and in this way you will fulfill the law of Christ. If anyone thinks he is something when he is nothing, he deceives himself. Each one should test his actions. Then he can take pride in himself, without comparing himself to somebody else, for each one should carry his own load (Greek 'phortion')."*
>
> **Galatians 6:2-5** (New International Version)

a. "Baros" defined: burden, trouble. When someone is carrying a heavy burden that is pressing down, they need help to carry it.

b. "Phortion" defined: a load. Each person must bear their own load because only they can bear it.

2. Challenges to not understanding healthy problem ownership:

    a. Many Christians are out to rescue the world and are more in touch with others' problems than they are with their own problems.

    b. Rescuing and owning other's problems can become addictive and can become a way of avoiding your self.

    c. When you incorrectly carry other's burdens, you are subject to burnout because you are carrying problems that are not your own.

3. If you take the problems of others and handle them, then you are treating that person as a child. This does not give them the opportunity to grow up. You may come across as controlling. Eventually the person who owns the problem will resent you and not want you to interfere in their life.

Which of these challenges do you struggle most with?

_____

_____

_____

_____

_____

_____

_____

4. In all the problems of life, one must decide **who really owns the problem**.

- **I own it:**
  If I own the problem, I must take action to solve the problem.
- **You own it:**
  If you own the problem, you must take action to solve the problem.
- **We own it:**
  If we own the problem, we must take action to solve the problem.
- **Nobody owns it:**
  If no one owns the problem, no solution is necessary.

Adapted from Gail Eillis of Lakewood Presbyterian Church in Lakewood, Ohio, has put together the following helpful checklists:

WHEN I FEEL RESPONSIBLE *for* OTHERS, I...
- fix
- protect
- rescue
- control
- carry their feelings
- don't listen

WHEN I FEEL RESPONSIBLE *to* OTHERS, I come alongside others by...
- showing empathy
- encouraging
- sharing
- confronting
- being sensitive
- listening

WHEN I FEEL RESPONSIBLE *for* OTHERS, I FEEL...
- tired
- anxious
- fearful
- liable

WHEN I FEEL RESPONSIBLE *to* OTHERS, I FEEL...
- relaxed
- free
- aware
- valued

WHEN I FEEL RESPONSIBLE *for* OTHERS, I am concerned with ...
- the solution
- the answer
- circumstances
- being right
- details
- performance

WHEN I FEEL RESPONSIBLE *to* OTHERS, I am concerned with ...
- relating person-to-person as equal to others
- listening to others feelings and thoughts
- respecting the person

Bottom Line:
- I am a manipulator
- I expect the person to live up to my expectations

Bottom Line:
- I am a helper/guide
- I can trust and let go

5. Five reasons why you get caught up in unhealthy problem ownership:

   a. Unhealed past issues. The past is not the past until you deal with it.

   b. Poor self-image.

   c. Ungodly beliefs (inner vows, Bitter Root Judgments, etc.)

   d. Codependent characteristics. Enabling behavior.

   e. Misconceptions of what is truth.

Which of these reasons cause you to get caught up in unhealthy relationships?

_____

_____

_____

_____

_____

_____

_____

_____

_____

_____

Jan Gossner, a theologian from Oslo, Norway has developed a survey that will help you look at yourself.

RESPONSIBILITY CHECKLIST

(Place the number that best describes your answer in the space provided.)

Total lack of Responsibility	Under Responsible	Peaceful, Relaxed, Responsible	Over Responsible	Hyper Responsible
1	2	3	4	5

1. As a child, I was _____.

2. Mother would say I was _____.

3. Dad would say I was _____.

4. My spouse, roommate or close friend would say I was _____.

5. I say I am at _____ today.

6. I want to be _____ as soon as possible.

Remember it is easy to become out of balance if you **react fast** and **think later**.

6. Correct/healthy problem ownership means:

   a. I'm responsible for my emotions.
      I'm not responsible for others emotions.

   b. I'm responsible for my thoughts.
      I'm not responsible for others thoughts.

   c. I'm responsible for my beliefs.
      I'm not responsible for others beliefs.

   d. I'm responsible for my actions.
      I'm not responsible for others actions.

   e. I'm responsible for me, and I only have the ability to change me.

   f. I'm not responsible for you, nor do I have the ability to change anything about you!

In what relationships do you most struggle with problem ownership?

_____

_____

_____

_____

_____

_____

_____

_____

_____

_____

"In everything, therefore, treat people the same way you want them to treat you."

Matthew 7:12 (NASV)

7. Using the acronym B.E.A.R., we can look at what scripture has to say about problem ownership:

   B = Bear – to stand beside and "bear watching" another handle their own pain.

   E = Empathy – to love someone unconditionally as they struggle *through* their problems. *"You seem to be_____(feeling)_____, are you?"*

   A = Action – to let go. Don't assume a person wants you to do something just because they are sharing with you.

   R = Respect – to walk beside the person and intercede for them.

8. Five steps to identify who owns the problem(s):

1. Listen. Many times you may be thinking of a response to make in conversation instead of really listening to the person who is talking. It is OK if there is silence in the conversation.

> *"My dear brothers, take note of this: Everyone should be quick to listen, slow to speak and slow to become angry."*
> **James 1:19 (NIV)**

2. Identify what is the real problem. Pretend that you are watching the event but the sound is on mute. You see the event but you cannot hear the event.
   a. *What are you seeing?* Then think about the emotions behind the words.
   b. *What do you believe about what you have heard?* Is your belief Biblically based? If not, what needs to be changed.

3. Clarify the situation by asking good questions. This discussion will help identify if you, the other person, or both of you own the problem. Perhaps no one owns the problem.

4. Delay. When you are not sure, take time out. Take the situation to God in prayer. Pray in the Spirit if you don't know how to pray for the situation.

> *"In the same way, the Spirit helps us in our weakness. We do not know what we ought to pray for, but the Spirit Himself intercedes for us with groans that words cannot express. And He who searches our hearts knows the mind of the Spirit, because the Spirit intercedes for the saints in accordance with God's will."*
> **Romans 8:26-27 (NIV)**

5. Affirm and Empower.
   If the problem is the other person's, affirm their ability to handle the situation. Pray for them and with them.

A goal in life should be to move toward peaceful, relaxed, and responsible relationships. When we trust in God we are able to let go of the issues that others need to deal with. A good rule of thumb is to ask yourself the question, ***"Will this issue make a difference with the eternal life of the person?"*** If the answer is "no", then perhaps the issue needs to be put into proper perspective.

You cannot own another's pain or unhealthy beliefs. You must point them to Jesus who has the healing and answers.

Exercises in Problem Ownership

Look over the examples to decide (a) what is the problem, and (b) who owns the problem.

1. Maria had an important appointment at 3:30 p.m. She goes out to start the car and it won't start. Maria becomes upset with her husband because husbands are to protect their wives by keeping their cars running smoothly.

   Problem _____

   Who owns it? _____

2. Jose and Ruth are having marriage problems. Ruth comes over and in tears asks you whether or not she should get a divorce.

   Problem _____

   Who owns it? _____

3. Willie has promised to take his family to a movie. The phone rings and on the other end is John, who is crying and obviously drunk. Willie knows that John is an alcoholic. Willie has

ministered to John many times before and has continued to pray for him, but John's been unwilling to face the truth. Willie told John not to call when he's been drinking.

Problem _____

Who owns it? _____

4. Diamond is responsible for all bill writing and keeping tabs on the checkbook. Henry, her husband, uses the "Anytime Bank" for withdrawals and neglects to tell Diamond. Their car payment is returned in the mail for lack of funds.

Problem _____

Who owns it? _____

5. Tyrone and Todd are roommates. At the beginning of the relationship it was agreed that Todd would clean and Tyrone would cook. Tyrone has kept his end of the agreement, but Todd hasn't cleaned since they moved in several months ago.

Problem _____

Who owns it? _____

6. Asia and Jane are your two best friends. Recently Asia lent Jane some money and expected to be paid back within a week. Jane has not paid Asia back, and she is angry at Jane because she needs the money to pay her car insurance. Asia has asked you to talk to Jane for her.

Problem _____

Who owns it? _____

7. Judy has become a very critical person concerning church. It seems like every time you get together, she criticizes the church leaders.

Problem _____

Who owns it? _____

See page 262 for the correct answers

Breakthrough Decrees (repeat daily)
(activate your words with body action)

1. I care about others and therefore allow them to own their own problems (Proverbs 19:19).

2. I trust in God and am able to let go of the issues that others need to deal with (Romans 8:26-27).

3. I listen to others before I speak and ask good questions (James 1:19).

4. I have the wisdom of God today. I will think the right thoughts, say the right words, and make the right decisions in every situation I face (James 1:5; 1 Corinthians 2:16).

5. I trust that God has my loved one's best interests in mind and He will lead, guide, and direct them. They make good decisions (Isaiah 40:11; Jeremiah 29:11).

6. My truth to replace the lie:_____

   On this day _____, I establish these decrees that are founded in God's Word.

Fill-in-the-Blank Answer Guide

Exercise answers
1. Maria
2. Ruth
3. Willie
4. both
5. Tyrone
6. Asia
7. Judy

Homework This Week

Think about a situation involving **conflict** that you either observed or were involved in this week. **Describe** the situation and **identify** problem ownership.

_____

_____

_____

_____

_____

_____

_____

_____

_____

_____

_____

_____

_____

Resources

I Don't Have to Make Everything All Better by Gary and Joy Lundberg, Penguin Books, 2000.

Personal Notes

Codependency Versus Interdependency

The more you've been hurt and the weaker your boundaries, the more you react strongly to people and events. If you have codependent tendencies you depend too much on others for your emotional health, self-worth, and identity. God wants your self-esteem based in THEIR identity for you, not what other people think.

Do your needs take a backseat to your beloved's or do you both consider each other's needs in meaningful ways? Knowing this can help you build a healthy marriage.

Is your relationship codependent or interdependent? To answer this, consider these statements:

1. "I need you. I can't live without you. You complete me." (Jerry Maguire movie)

2. "I want you. We make a great team. I'm glad you're my spouse."

"But wait, shouldn't I want someone to feel like they can't live without me and that I complete them?" No

These are common signs of codependency:

- You rely excessively on the other for your emotional well-being, self-worth, and identity. Your self-esteem comes from outside yourself and that's not healthy for either of you.

- You're enmeshed in each other's lives to an unhealthy extent. For example, your mood, emotions, and decision-making ability are governed by the feelings, behavior, or responses of your beloved (or a family member or friend).

- You have an inability to function independently. You may even struggle to make decisions or take actions without seeking validation or permission from your spouse.

Interdependence is very different. Signs include:

- You are two autonomous individuals who make a choice to be together and form a couple. I don't complete you but I do choose you. You share a strong connection with each other but you don't control the other.

- You find personal fulfillment through your own interests, friendships, and activities. You enjoy your beloved but you are your own person as well.

- There's a healthy give-and-take dynamic, where both spouses contribute to the relationship and support each other's separate growth and well-being.

Beware of falling into the trap of Independence which often ends as "married singles". You live life independent of each other, each doing your own thing. It can feel like you are simply roommates. It's a relationship of convenience but not of intimacy. It is an easy path to go down particularly if you both have unhealed trauma.

 **Resources**

Boundaries Updated and Expanded Edition: When to Say Yes. How to Say No To Take Control of Your Life. October 3, 2017. Henry Cloud and John Townsend.

Additional Resources

Telling Yourself the Truth, William Backus, Ph.D., Bethany House Publishing 1985.

Who Am I and Why Am I Here, Dr. Bill Hamon, Destiny Image Publishing, 2005.

Activating You to Heal the Sick: Masterclass Workbook, Patti Hathaway, M.Ed., Breakthrough Hope & Healing, 2020.

I Don't Have to Make Everything All Better, Gary and Joy Lundberg, Penguin Books, 2000.

The Handbook for Spiritual Warfare, Dr. Ed Murphy, Thomas Nelson Publishers, 1992.

Healing the Wounded Spirit, John and Paula Sandford, Bridge Publishing, 1985.

Other Prayer Resources:

Freemasonry and other religions:
https://jubileeresources.org/?page_id=86

Authority Prayers from Erin Lamb:
https://ithoughtiknewwhatlovewas.com/authority-prayers/

Prayers from Rev. Annie Aakelian:
http://lightofthecomforter.org/prayers/

Authors

Patti Hathaway, M.Ed. is a Certified Speaking Professional, Coach and Mentor for 25+ years. She is the author of eight books and seven online programs. Her books have collectively sold more than 100,000 copies worldwide. Patti was the COO for 2 entrepreneurial companies and she now serves as the CEO and Steward of a humanitarian foundation.

Patti and her husband Jim have been through the good, bad, and ugly in 40 years of marriage and she shares authentically and vulnerably how to survive and thrive through it all with the help of Jesus. They raised two incredible young adult sons.

When Patti says "I feel your pain" she really does feel your pain. She's been there, and done that. God will come through for you two because He loves to do the impossible. In Matthew 17:20 Jesus said, "Truly I tell you, if you have faith as small as a mustard seed, you can say to this mountain, 'Move from here to there,' and it will move. Nothing will be impossible for you."

Patti's specialty is masterfully teaching couples how to heal their soul (their mind, will and emotions) so they get back to having incredible, love-filled marriages. People are healed inside and out.

Contact Patti at PattiHath@G4U.Foundation
G4U Foundation, S.A.
1985 W. Henderson Rd, #3127
Columbus, Ohio 43220

You can learn more about Patti at her websites:
www.G4U.Foundation
www.SoulHealingCourses.com
www.HumanTraffickingElearning.com
www.TheChangeAgent.com

Keren Anderson was born in Brazil to missionary parents. She possesses a global perspective on Kingdom Transformation. Fueled by a deep-seated passion and equipped with certifications as a Coach, Trauma Counselor, SOZO Trainer, and Chaplain, she is dedicated to aiding those affected by trauma. Drawing from her diverse experiences, Keren has established a transformative ministry.

Her focus lies in providing support to individuals who have encountered various forms of abuse, with a particular emphasis on childhood abuse. Keren aspires to establish treatment centers across every county in Ohio, with the ultimate goal of creating a replicable model for global implementation. As a dual citizen of Brazil and the USA, she nurtures relationships across numerous countries.

Beyond her humanitarian efforts, Keren serves as a teacher, writer, and pastor to individuals seeking holistic well-being. Additionally, she imparts her knowledge as a trainer to those eager to contribute to the healing of a world in need. A mother to four married children, she is a proud Mimi to thirteen grandchildren and eight great-grandchildren.

Contact Keren at D4Hiam@proton.me
D4H Foundation, S.A.
46 S. James Road, #2012
Columbus, Ohio 43213

Website: www.D4H.Foundation